Scientometric Indicators And Webometrics - And The Polyrepresentation Principle In Information Retrieval

Scientometric Indicators and Webometrics – And the Polyrepresentation Principle In Information Retrieval

By

PETER INGWERSEN

Professor Emeritus, D. Ph. (Honoris causa).
Royal School of Library and Information Science
Birketinget 6, DK 2300 Copenhagen S – Denmark

and

Professor II, Department of Archive, Library and Information Science
Oslo University College, St. Olavs Plass, 0130 Oslo – Norway

Published By

Ess Ess Publications
New Delhi
for

Sarada Ranganathan Endowment for Library Science
Bangalore

Sarada Ranganathan Endowment Lectures (28) (2010)

S.R. Ranganathan's
Five Laws of Library Science

Books are for Use
Every Reader his/her Book
Every Book its Reader
Save the Time of the Reader
Library is a Growing Organism

ISBN: 978-81-7000-657-2

Ess Ess
Rs.475/-
First Published 2012

Published by:
Ess Ess Publications
4837/24, Ansari Road,
Darya Ganj,
New Delhi-110 002.
INDIA
Phones: 23260807, 41563444
Fax: 41563334
E-mail: info@essessreference.com
www.essessreference.com

for

Sarada Ranganathan Endowment for Library Science
702, 'Upstairs', 42nd Cross, III Block, Rajajinagar,
Bangalore-560 010
E-mail: srels@dataone.in Phone: 080-23305109

Printed and bound in India at Salasar Imaging Systems.

Contents

Preface

What cannot be measured cannot be quantified; what cannot be quantified cannot be controlled; what cannot be controlled, cannot be managed! According to William Thompson (Lord Kelvin), "if something cannot be measured, then it cannot be improved;" often quoted it as 'if it cannot be measured, then it is not science'. In the last five decades, it has been realized that measuring scientific outputs in the field of science and technology is not only a necessity, but also the means to make sense of the complexity of scientific activities. In this process, several indicators have been developed to assess 'science and technology outputs'. Such indicators are known as scientometric indicators and they are used to identify strengths and weakness of an entity; the entity may be an individual, institution, journal or country; they describe the state of the entire scientific endeavor. Some simple indicators are number of papers published (by individuals, institutions, countries, journals, etc.), growth and obsolescence rates, impact factor, activity index, collaboration index, R & D expenditure, etc. These indicators are useful in:

- Analyzing research performance of institutions, countries and individuals,
- Identifying research trends
- Ranking journals, scientists, papers, institutions and countries in a given field of research

- Evaluating scientists, institutions, reviewers, journals, etc.

In the recent past, in Scandinavian countries, Crown Indicators were developed. They are relative impact indicators for a given entity that are normalized in relation to the research fields globally. There are two such indicators – Journal Crown Indicators (JCI) and Field Crown Indicators (FCI). The JCI is defined as the ratio between the number of citations received by a given unit and the diachronic citation impact of the corresponding journals used by the unit during a given period. The FCI is defined as the ratio between the number of citations received by a given unit and the global diachronic citation impact weighted according to the research profiles displayed by the unit during the same period. These are well discussed in the first lecture.

Dr Ingwersen in his first lecture discusses two basic models of scientific communication – the one prior to the Web and the other one Internet-based model, which includes open access to information. This is followed by a discussion on selected central publication and citation-based indicators, including the Crown Indicators, for research evaluation. He also discusses the Scandinavian Bibliometric Indicators (generally known as Publication Point Indicator). He points out that it may correspond to citation impact in a research institution, leading to a combined point and citation impact.

The second lecture is on webometrics. According to Bjorneborn and Ingwersen, webometrics deals with the quantitative aspects of the construction and use of information resources, structure and technologies on the Web. Its scope includes search engine performance, link structures, users' information seeking behavior (on the Web), web page content, etc. He further talks on the potentials of webometrics ranging from search engine and link analysis, web impact factor, etc. to a discussion of new scientific data set usage indicators.

In the past, researchers in the area of information retrieval developed strategies to increase recall and precision for a given query. In order to increase recall, one may use synonyms or broader terms or limiting the use of the Boolean "and" or search both "natural language fields" (e.g. titles and abstracts) and "controlled fields". Similarly, precision might be improved by delimiting the search to certain fields (e.g. titles, descriptors, and identifiers). It was also well known among experienced researchers that one can increase precision by searching a word that represents in more than one field (e.g., the term retrieval may be searched both in titles and descriptors.). This is termed as "polyrepresentation" and "cognitive overlaps" by Ingwersen in his earlier works and claimed to be a theory and part of "a cognitive view" in IR. The concept of polyrepresentation is not new and Ingwersen has contributed much in this area. His third lecture is concentrated on polyrepresentation. Some see polyrepresentation as a theory of information retrieval. It also points to a variety of empirical studies related to IR. He further discusses the empirical investigations that are directly founded on polyrepresentation principles, ideas and assumptions, which illustrate polyrepresentation in detail.

Dr. Ingwrsen, in the series of three lectures covers interesting and the more important topics in informetrics. This document will certainly be useful for researchers and students in informetrics.

Bangalore
7 July 2011

I.K. Ravichandra Rao
Professor
Documentation Research and Training Centre
Indian Statistical Institute, Bangalore.

Foreword

The Sarada Ranganathan Endowment for Library Science (SRELS), founded by Dr. S.R. Ranganathan in 1961, is registered as a Charitable Endowment with the Government of India (1963).

The aims of the Endowment briefly are:

- To improve the library and information services in India
- To train library and information service personnel
- To promote the provision of efficient library and information service
- To apply research results to library and information studies

The objectives of the Endowment are:

- Furthering the cause of library and information service
- Organising Seminars and Workshops on recent developments in library and information science and the related fields.
- Organising periodically courses of lectures on recent developments in library and information science and related fields by national and international experts
- Supporting the publication of these lectures and of other nascent ideas in the field of library and information science.

The Endowment is furthering these objectives by publishing a periodical entitled SRELS Journal of Information Management (formerly, Library Science with a slant to Documentation (from 1964 to 1988), and Library Science with slant to Documentation and Information Studies (from 1988 to 1999). Workshops, Lecture presentations and Seminars are also organized periodically.

There are three series of lectures organized under the auspices of the Endowment:

1. Sarada Ranganathan Endowment Lectures. (1965-);
2. Dr. S.R. Ranganathan Memorial Lectures. (1973-); and
3. Curzon-Seshachalam Endowment Lectures. (2001-).

Scientometric Indicators, Webometrics and Polyrepresentation is the text of the ***28th Sarada Ranganathan Endowment Lectures*** delivered by ***Dr. Peter Ingwersen,*** Professor, 'Royal' School of Library and Information Science, Copenhagen, Denmark on 8, 9 and 10 December 2010 in Bangalore.

The lecture on Scientometric indicators presented two fundamental models of scientific communication – the classic one mainly providing access to document records in library catalogues and bibliographic databases, and the digitized one, relying on open access and diversified document access potentials. The lecture contextualizes, characterizes and exemplifies the concept of 'Scientometrics'.

The second lecture on the Range of Webometrics provides insights into the history of webometrics in context of other research evaluation methods. The lecture exemplifies selected cases, both from traditional webometric analyses and new ones based on scientific dataset usage and comparisons of link and download/reading patterns for newspapers.

The third lecture is on Poly-representation which provides on integrated and explicitly cognitive framework for understanding the process involved in Information Retrieval. The lecture outline the principle of poly-representation with a focus on the kinds of representations involved. The potentials, strengths and problems of applying the principle are discussed in the light of recent studies. The challenges and opportunities for future research are indentified along a Poly-representation Continuum.

Bangalore
7 July 2011

K.N. Prasad
Executive Officer
Sarada Ranganathan Endowment for Library Science

Acknowledgements

I am grateful to the Board of Trustees of the Sarada Ranganathan Endowment for Library Science (SRELS) for providing me with the opportunity to deliver the Sarada Ranganathan Endowment Lectures 2010. In particular, I am grateful to Professor I.K. Ravichandra Rao, Documentation Research and Training Centre, Indian Statistical Institute, for his warm support prior to and during my visit and valuable suggestions preparing this document. I also wish to thank Professor A. Neelameghan, SRELS, and Professor K.S. Raghavan, Documentation Research and Training Centre, Indian Statistical Institute, for their helpful input during my lecturing. I am also very thankful to Dr. K.N. Prasad, Executive Officer, SRELS, for all the support he has given me. Finally, I wish to express my appreciation to the many students for their constant eagerness and helpfulness.

PETER INGWERSEN

Professor Emeritus, D.Ph. (Honoris causa)

Royal School of Library and Information Science

Copenhagen, Denmark

About The Author

Peter Ingwersen is Professor Emeritus (2010), the Royal School of Library and Information Science (RSLIS), Copenhagen, Denmark, where he served as Professor of Information Science from 2001. Currently he working as Affiliate Professor at the Oslo University College, Norway and is also Visiting Professor at Abo Akademi University, Turku, Finland.

Professor Ingwersen was born in 1947 and became lecturer at RSLIS in 1973, after graduation from the School in the same year. He obtained his Ph.D. degree 1991 from Copenhagen Business School, Faculty of Economics, Institute of Informatics and Management with a doctoral dissertation on Intermediary Functions in Information Retrieval Interaction. In May 2010 he was awarded the degree D. Ph. Honoris Causa by the Information Science Faculty of University of Tampere, Finland.

Until 1982 he lectured on information storage and retrieval, cataloguing and indexing theory and carried out research on cognitive aspects of information seeking and retrieval. In 1982-84 he joined the online service staff of the Information Retrieval Service, the European Space Agency (ESA-IRS), Frascati, Italy, as ESA Research Fellow. His R & D activities were concerned with user-system interface improvements, the development of a new family of online support and retrieval tools, like the Zoom/RANK command facility, as well as systems management.

Back at RSLIS as Associate Professor from 1984, he worked in a new department dealing with IRM and design of specialized information services and systems for industry and institutions. As the driving force behind the curriculum development of the M.Sc. program in Library and Information Science at RSLIS he was appointed head of this program 1990-93. From July 1993 he became Head of the Department of Information Retrieval Theory, in 1999 merged with Department of Information Studies. He was senior researcher at the Centre for Informetric Studies (CIS), RSLIS, 1996-2000. From January 2001 he became Research Professor, called as full professor in that deperatment 2005, specializing in Information Seeking, Interactive Information Retrieval, and Informetrics/Webometrics. Retired from RSLIS in August 2010 as Professor Emeritus.

During the Spring-term 1987 he served as Visiting Professor at Rutgers University, NJ, USA, invited by the School of Communication, Information and Library Studies. He has been Visiting Scholar at Keio University, Tokyo, Japan, 1996 and at University of Pretoria, Republic of South Africa, 1997, one month in each institution. In 1999-2002 he served as Visiting Professor at the Department of Information Studies, Tampere University, Finland, sponsored by the Nordic Research Academy (Norfa), now named NORDFORSK. He was invited as Visiting Scholar by Shanghai Library and China Academy of Science, the Documentation and Information Center, Shanghai in August, 2003 – and once again in 2008. He is member of the Advisory Board of the International Collaborative Academy of Library and Information Science (ICALIS), Wuhan University, from 2008.

From January 1997 he is appointed and serves as Affiliate Professor (Docent) at Åbo Akademi University,

Department of Information Studies, Turku, Finland and from October 2010 he is Professor II at Oslo University College, Norway, with 20 % academic duties.

Among his published works are several research monographs on information retrieval, as well as more than 100 peer reviewed journal, conference and book articles on information science, curriculum development, information systems design, informetrics, including research evaluation and Webometric analyses, and, in particular, on integrated cognitive approaches to interactive IR theory. Together with the late Thomas Almind he coined the notion of Webometrics, signifying the quantitative studies of the WWW. He has contributed articles on information science and retrieval to the Encyclopedia of Library and Information Science, USA, 1995 and 2010. His first monograph, Information Retrieval Interaction, 1992, has sold more than 2000 copies worldwide and is also published in Japanese translation, 1995, as well as in Korean, 1998 and Persian, 2010. It is available free on the web from 2002, and has been visited almost 17,000 times.

Together with Academy Professor Kalervo Järvelin, Tampere University, Finland, he published in 2005 (by Springer) his most recent monograph: *The Turn: Integration of Information Seeking and Retrieval in Context,* which has been translated into Chinese by ISTIC, Beijing, 2007 and Japanese by Maruzen Publishers, 2008.

His is currently engaged in a variety of research evaluation studies and in the *I*-Search Project at RSLIS concerned with integrated retrieval and the research developments of polyrepresentation principle.

As expert consultant he has served in several ESPRIT projects on the design of knowledge-based IR interfaces and systems, and participated in the development of the information system of the Danish Parliament. Professor Ingwersen served as EU reviewer on ESPRIT and Basic

Research (LTR) projects (SIMPR; FERMI), and he participated in the three-year ESPRIT Long Term Research consortium (MIRA) developing evaluation methods for interactive multi-media retrieval, sponsored by the EU Commission.

He has been Chair or member of three international university departmental research assessment committees, most recently as panel member at the departmental and centre evaluation 2008 of CWTS, Leiden University, The Netherlands. Since 1993 he has been member of 18 professorial evaluation committees and official external examiner at 18 doctoral examinations.

Since 2000 Prof. Ingwersen has supervised 7 doctoral theses on interactive IR, Citation-based IR, Webometrics and Small World phenomena, Thesaurus design and use, Collaborative information seeking and Informetric methods applied to thesaurus design as well as on Museum taxonomies for cultural heritage. He has supervised long-term visiting Chinese, Japanese, Spanish and UK post-doctoral and doctoral researchers and visiting professors. From 1998 he has organized several one and two-week international doctoral research courses, on Information Seeking and Retrieval (ISR) and Informetrics, sponsored by the Nordic Academy of Research (NORFA), and has participated in several Nordic and EU sponsored PhD courses and summer schools (e.g. ESSIR from 1999).

He was member of the Standing Executive Committees of the NORFA-sponsored research network for Information Studies: NORDISNet 1998-2002 with 1.5 Mill. NOK, the ensuing Nordic research school, NORSLIS, 2004-2008, sponsored by NordForsk with 1 Mill NOK/year, and the South African research educational network DISSANet 1998-2000 sponsored by DANIDA with 2.6 Mill. DKK.

As Conference Chairman he organized the 15th ACM-SIGIR Conference on RandD in Information Retrieval, held in Copenhagen, June 1992, and co-chaired the CoLIS 2-4 Conferences on Conceptions of Library and Information Science, held in Copenhagen, 1996, Dubrovnik, Croatia, 1999, and Seattle, USA, 2002. Since 1989 he is member of the ACM-SIGIR international Program Committee, and served as its EU Program Chair 1995 and 2000. He was member of the editorial board of *Journal of Documentation* 1990-2001, and is currently board member of the *Journal of American Society of Information Science and Technology* (JASIST), *Scientometrics, Journal of Informetrics, Information Processing and Management, Chinese Journal of Science and Technology Information, South African Journal of Library and Information Science*, and the electronic journal *Cybermetrics*.

Prof. Ingwersen has received several awards and research medals. He received the Jason Farradane Award, 1993 from the Institute of Information Scientists, UK. In 1994 he received the American Society for Information Science/ New Jersey Distinguished Lectureship Award, and in 2003 the distinguished American Society for Information Science and Technology (ASISandT) Research Award, for his work on the cognitive approach to Information Retrieval. In 2005 he was honored by the Thomson Award of excellence in Denmark, being the most highly internationally cited Danish researcher in the social sciences. That same year he received the prestigious Derek De Solla Price Award, selected by the international peers in Scientometrics and Informetrics. In 2007 ASISandT awarded him the Outstanding Information Science Teacher Award. In 2009 the Los Angeles Chapter of ASISandT awarded him with the Contributions to Information Science and Technology Award (CISTA). Among his invited lectures and key-notes worldwide are the Anne V. Marinelli Lecture Series, Texas Woman's University, 1992 as well as the Lazarow Memorial Lecture twice: 1) The Information School, University of Washington, Seattle, 2002, and 2) University of Tennessee, 2009, sponsored by Thomson Reuters and the Eugene Garfield Foundation.

Introduction

Don Swanson, the former Dean of the Chicago School of Library and Information Science, once told me that I was lucky to be dealing with both interactive Information Retrieval (IR) *and* Bibliometrics. Like he himself had done I might profit from the many interesting information structures and methodologies known from the latter when pursuing research in the former. This is one of the reasons why I did chose to mix presentations of Scientometric indicators and Webometric analyses, with a lecture on polyrepresentation in IR.

A mathematical bridge exists between informetric analyses and IR: Bradford's Law adhering to the former and Zipf's Law, the basis for automatic indexing in IR, are closely related regularities of frequency rank distributions. Other central mathematical models are also in common, for instance, the vector space and cosine models applied to author co-citation (and other kinds of) mapping in scientometrics and as retrieval principles in IR. Most obvious is the PageRank Web search algorithm by Brin and Page (1998). PageRank in Google and similar retrieval models in other web search engines are partly based on the assumption that web links are 'like' academic citations: the more inlinks a webpage obtains and the 'better' or more 'recognized' it is – the higher it should be placed on the retrieval ranking. Since

PageRank is iterative a self-reinforcing mechanism assures that a page linked to from webpages with a high PageRank also obtains a high PageRank. This algorithm is mathematically nice and successful in web engines for known-item and fact searching - but the underlying assumption is false. Links are *not* 'like' academic citations (or references) and a high PageRank *does not* assure a high level of topical or situational 'relevance' as understood in IR. In the same way 'many citations' do not necessarily assure usefulness or pertinence of documents retrieved and sorted by citations, e.g. as done in Google Scholar or Web of Science. In fact, how to apply academic citations in IR is not well understood.

In my lectures I will only sporadically deal with web search engines, and then only for the purpose of Webometric analyses. However, the reasons why I connect Scientometrics (and the informetric sub-field of Webometrics) with IR in my lectures are three-fold:

1. *Information Retrieval techniques* are mandatory for carrying out data capturing for Scientometric (and Webometric) analyses.

2. *All representations* of *documents, their features* and their *relationships*, also known from informetrics, are potentially useful in IR - including citations (to documents); references (from documents); particular content elements and features like anchor texts, terms, other content keys, metadata, etc. representing documents, and vice versa; link structures; (co-) authorships; journal (and other carrier) names; etc.

3. *New social utility tools and representations*, known from Web 2.0 applications and IR in social media, also provide novel and potentially forceful indicators of use.

Common IR techniques are well known in the Scientometric research community, whether in traditional online domain-based searching (Christensen and Ingwersen,

1997), in Web of Science or Scopus (Moed, 2005), Google Scholar (Jacso, 2008) or on the Web in general (Thelwall et al., 2005).

The first two lectures do not deal with such techniques, but with the specialized *information derived from searching* dedicated Scientometric and Webometric indicator analysis and calculation. In particular the social utility representations, such as data captured on rating, recommendation or social tagging of information entities, Webpage visits and downloads or topic density in blogs, etc., have great potential as elements of novel often Web-based indicators (Elleby and Ingwersen, 2010).

The third lecture, however, explicitly takes up the principle of polyrepresentation (2005; 2009; 2010), which makes use of the *variety of representations* of documents and document features, including references and citations, with the purpose of improving IR performance.

Lecture 1 is titled "Scientometric Indicators – Into Open Access and Publication Points for Research Evaluation". It attempts first to outline fundamental models for scientific communication, which increasingly include open access to information but also demonstrate higher complexity as to quality separation. This is followed by outlining and exemplification of central publication and citation indicators, including typical Crown Indicators. Samples are from large developing countries like India and China as well as from small developed countries like Denmark and Switzerland. The so-called "publication point" indicator applied to the distribution of the governmental financial support to RandD in Norway and Denmark is described and compared to citation impact for a multidisciplinary research institution.

Lecture 2, "The Range of Webometrics – Forms of Digital Social Utility as Tools", deals with the definition of Webometric analysis and link terminology. It demonstrates selected analyses of search engine performance, the Web

Impact Factor and its drawbacks, comparisons between links and references (citations), and exemplifies social utility tools by presenting new indicators for scientific (biodiversity) dataset usage and blog analysis

Lecture 3 is named "Polyrepresentation - Bridging Laboratory Information Retrieval and User Context". Initially it defines the conception and principle of polyrepresentation and describes its underlying hypothesis. The lecture then outlines the empirical evidence behind the principle from two perspectives. One approach discusses evidence from experiments that are not explicitly based on the principle, but carried out in other theoretical contexts. The second perspective analyses the evidence from experiments and studies, which are explicitly founded on the principle of polyrepresentation. We distinguish between polyrepresentation of the information space, the IR interaction process and the cognitive space, and point to possible future research scenarios.

1

Scientometric Indicators: Into Open Access And Publication Points For Research Evaluation

In this lecture I will first outline the two basic models of scientific communication: the traditional pre-Internet model and the more complex open access (OA) and Internet-based model. This is followed by a discussion and exemplification of selected central publication and citation-based indicators for research evaluation, including the so-called Crown Indicators. The lecture ends with a discussion of the recent development of the so-called Publication (success) Point Indicators – the Scandinavian Bibliometric Indicator – and how it may correspond to citation impact in a real research institution, leading to a combined point-and-citation impact indicator. The lecture is complementary to that by I.K. Ravichandra Rao (2008).

SCIENTIFIC COMMUNICATION

The traditional or 'classic' model of scientific communication (De Solla Price) in the sciences and some social sciences is outlined in Fig. 1. To the left the research idea and efforts surface, which may take years to fulfill. During that period or at the end the classic model commonly incorporates a technical report stage. Simultaneously, the researcher(s) may produce initial results in the form of conference papers, abstracts or posters. The mode is domain-dependent. In the Computer or Information Science fields heavily peer reviewed conference papers and posters are preferred. In Medicine conference abstracts are used but not recognized as serious publication channels. Technical reports were traditionally seen as the backbone of research because they contain the bulk of the empirical data and theoretical-methodological approaches to the research project.

One line of communication was to send the report by snail mail to colleagues worldwide. This line is not peer reviewed, informal and the report not regarded as published in the real sense of the word - although they often form part of an institutional 'report series' - recently also seen as series of 'working papers'. The *printed* report is then archived in the institutional library.

The technical report (and the conference communications) might then be applied as stepping stones for journal article submissions. The time frame might easily be 1-2 years after the project ended prior to publication of the first peer reviewed journal article from the research project. When published the full text can be read in the journal itself. The only access to the article would be through poor metadata in a library index or more rich (and costly) domain databases that include abstracts. Finally, citation databases such as Thomson-Reuter's ISI Science Citation Index (SCI) or the Social Science Citation Index (SSCI) might index the article, if the publishing journal is regarded central to a research field by ISI. Approximately 25 % of the global peer reviewed journals are indexed in the ISI citation databases (Ulrich).

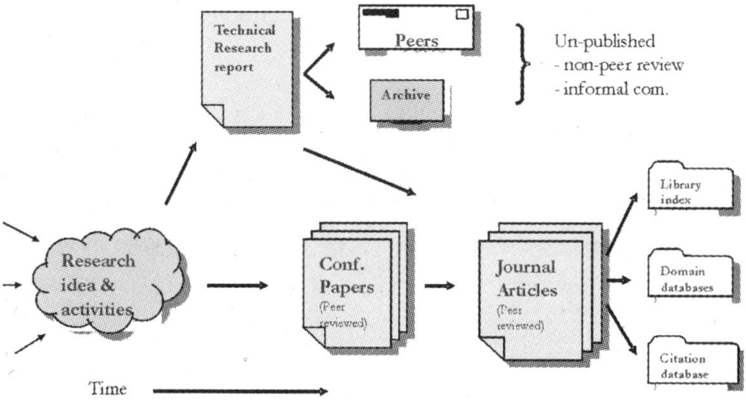

Fig. 1. Classic model of scientific communication – prior to the Web and open access.

THE WEB-BASED AND OPEN ACCESS BASED MODEL

The present model of scientific communication looks like Fig. 2. The technical report (or working paper) is still present; but now in electronic form and thus easily distributed by e-mail to peers.

Like previously the report is not peer reviewed and unpublished but public and often accessible in full text through an electronic *institutional repository*. In contrast to the era prior to the Internet the research activities may lead to immediate publications in peer reviewed OA journals, which commonly have a shorter reviewing and publication period compared to more traditional printed journals. Owing to OA principles the full text article can be legally stored also in the institutional repositories. The article may potentially be accessible through several repositories, depending on the authors' institutional affiliations.

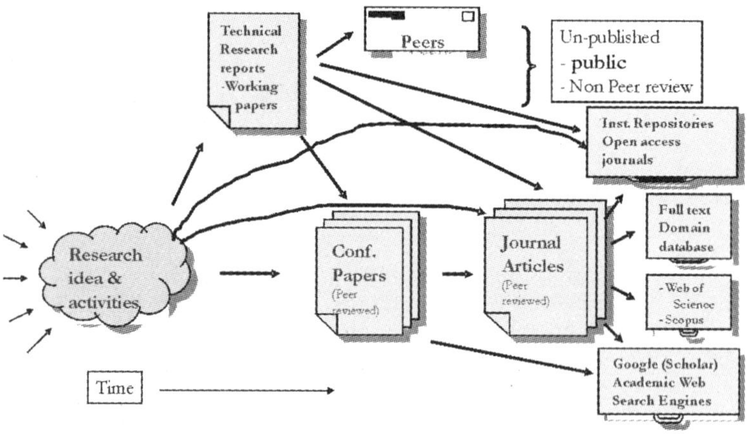

Fig. 2. Scientific communication model – in the age of the Internet and open access.

One may still see research reports and conference communications used as stepping stones for journal article submissions; but increasingly the direct line of communication is preferred by scientists. The end product (after acceptance and formal publication) is a full text article or conference paper/poster available through the repositories, the domain-related databases, such as arXiv.org (Physics; Computer Science), Medline or PubMed (Health Sciences), the citation databases (Web of Science and Scopus), or through the Web search engines, like Google (Scholar or Books), Yahoo or Bing.

In the Humanities and some Social Science fields the traditional model of communication prevails although the digitized possibility of publication is available. Commonly the *monograph* is the preferred vehicle of communication, replacing the conference papers and journal articles, and technical reports do rarely exist. Blindfolded peer reviewing is not common; if carried out reviewing is instead done by journal or book series editors. Access to the monographic contents is difficult because commonly still only scarce metadata through library records are used as access points. Increasingly monographic materials can be found through Google Books and in institutional repositories; but the coverage is less and more uncertain compared to the other vehicles of academic communication.

Because an increasing amount of information produced is in digitized format, scientific and quasi-scientific information become mixed together in repositories, databases and on the Web (Allen) (Jepsen). Fig. 3 outlines a typical selection of document types that makes future scientometric analyses cumbersome.

The diagram separates the information into two different kinds: *Qualified knowledge sources* (domain dependent) – the right-hand side; and *sources with degrees of* (academic) *confidence* assigned to them.

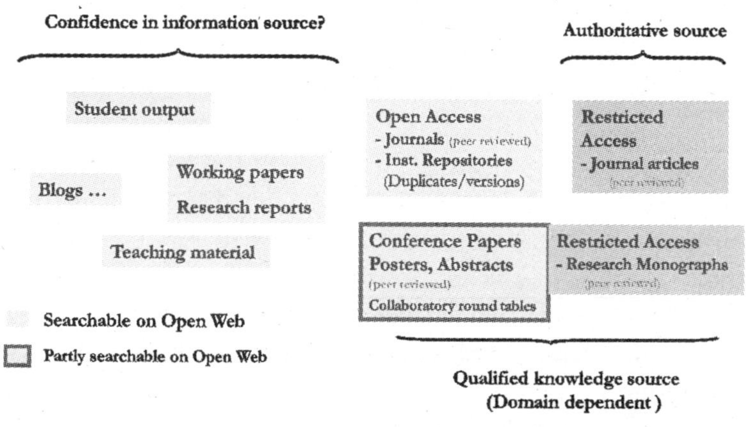

Fig. 3. The typical mixture of scientifically authoritative and qualified knowledge sources and more dubious information from a scientific stand.

The latter sources contain student theses at various levels; academic blogs; non-peer reviewed working papers and reports; teaching materials, like power point presentations, course literature and syllabi. Obviously, Ph.D. dissertations are seen as truly academic work; but what about M.Sc. and BA theses? Where goes the borderline? Academic blogs: they are not peer reviewed and often provide sheer opinions, not necessarily facts in an academic sense. Teaching materials: does a presentation of a lecture or a course program count as 'publications'?

The issue here is that all such kinds of information are searchable on the Web together with OA journal articles and a lot of other peer reviewed output often duplicated in institutional repositories (light gray area, Fig. 3). The problem is to *distinguish* between non-academic material and scientifically acceptable information, both at local and at global levels. With local repositories easily at hand the human trend will be to add as much 'material' into them as possible in order to demonstrate and boost own academic capacity and output, both as single scientist and as institution.

This is probably the reason why the *Authoritative sources*, Fig. 3, with their restricted (and often costly) access, still are the preferred ones in the case of serious research evaluation. These sources form part of the *hidden Web*. An alternative modus is to produce a national academic authority database, as done in Norway in connection with their Publication Point Indicator (Schneider). That database includes all published Norwegian monographs, articles and conference papers with duplicates removed and controlled metadata.

In summary, one may in general foresee a much higher degree of *cumbersome complexity* with respect to source definition and qualification in connection with future research evaluation activities at local (institutional), regional, national and global levels. Current and future information professionals will have a great responsibility in association with proper indexing of and distinction between the increasing variety information types and carriers.

PUBLICATION ANALYSIS - EXAMPLES

This section exemplifies some important publication indicators of the many in existence at present. A comprehensive discussion of publication analysis and indicators is provided by Moed (2005). In general publication analysis serves the purpose of counting *qualified* scientific publications in academic fields or disciplines (when defined), Fig. 3; in countries, regions, universities, departments, research groups; or over particular media, like journals or datasets, and over selected periods in the form of time series. Other kinds of document representations may also be analyzed, e.g. co-author density, international cooperation or acknowledgements.

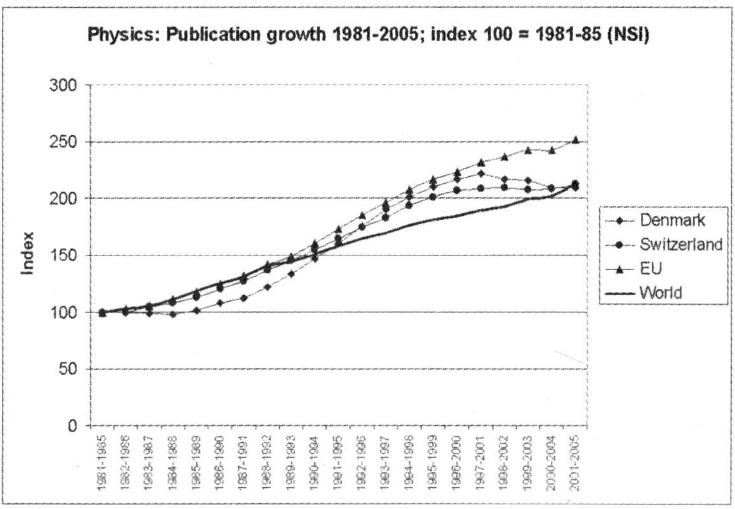

Fig. 4. Data based on National Science Indicators, 2006.

The output of publication analyses is quite descriptive in nature. However, more analytic and informative rank distributions are possible to create, based on the publication data (Rao, 2008). Such distributions may cover most productive countries, institutions, research groups or journals in a field, resulting in Bradford-like exponential distributions with typical 'long tails' (Heidorn). Other distributions take the form of time series, e.g. for comparative publication growth in Physics 1981-2005, Fig. 4.

We observe in Fig. 4, how the global (USA-dominated) and EU productivity are steadily growing whilst the Swiss (CERN) and Danish (Niels Bohr Institute) growth have stagnated or is falling in the 2000-05 period. Physicists maintain that they are awaiting the new ultra-large cyclotron at CERN to start its activities. This demonstrates that the analytic results often can only be explained by the domain experts (the researchers) themselves, not by informetricians!

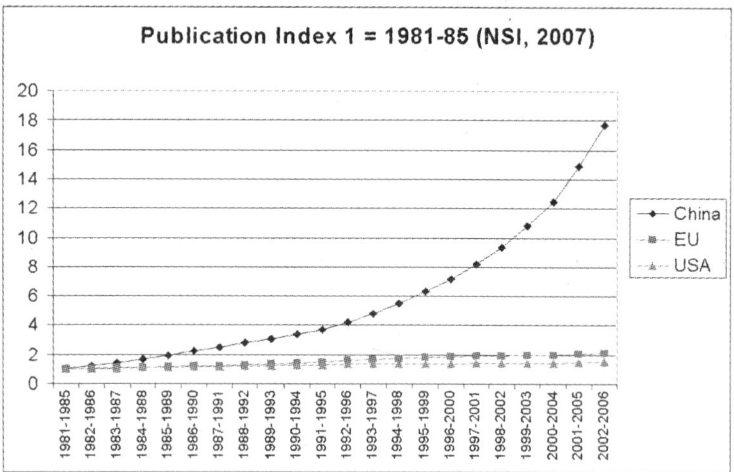

Fig. 5. Publication growth, all fields, in ISI citation databases. National Science Indicators, 2007. Index 1: 14,114 publ. (China); 736,616 publ. (EU); 887,037 publ. (USA).

Fig. 4 displays a typical index-based diagram, with the starting period (1981-85) as its initial index value (100). Fig. 5 does the same; but without any contextual knowledge the interpretation of the diagram would be totally biased! The eighteen-fold growth for China, compared to the steady development of EU and USA, does *not* mirror the *real growth* by Chinese sciences. It demonstrates solely the growth of Chinese publications indexed by the ISI citation databases over the period 1981-2006! It may thus show the increase of the *international visibility* of the Chinese sciences, that is, the growth of Chinese research published in principal international journals starting with 14,114 publications in the citation databases. This figure should be compared to those for USA and EU and India (65,250 publ.).

CITATION ANALYSIS

Like in publication analysis citation analyses may produce rank distributions of various kinds as well as *absolute* or *relative citation impact* indicators of selected research units, such as countries, regions, institutions, departments, research groups, subject fields or journals, datasets and other information carriers, etc. *Citedness,* i.e. the ratio of publications having received at least one citation during a given time window, is also an important indicator. Citation impact analyses presuppose that the corresponding publication analyses have been done.

Fundamentally two modes of citation analysis exist. The *diachronic* analysis, which analyses the citation development *forward* in time from a defined starting point (Ingwersen+Rousseau); the *synchronous* analysis mode, which observes the citation development *backwards* in time from a given starting point. Diachronic citation analysis is applied to the Crown Indicators discussed below. The well-known Journal Impact Factor (JIF), published annually by the Journal Citation Report as a part of Web of Science (Thomson-Reuters), is an example of a synchronous analysis: the number of citations received by a journal in year Y from all other sources to the articles, notes and review articles published by that journal in years Y-1 plus Y-2.

The *diachronic* analyses observe how older research is received (used or recognized) by recent research. By using Web of Science or Scopus (Elsevier) the analyses assure that only peer reviewed qualified information sources are included. Fig. 6 displays the developments of EU, USA and China of absolute impact, corresponding to the publication analysis shown Fig. 5.

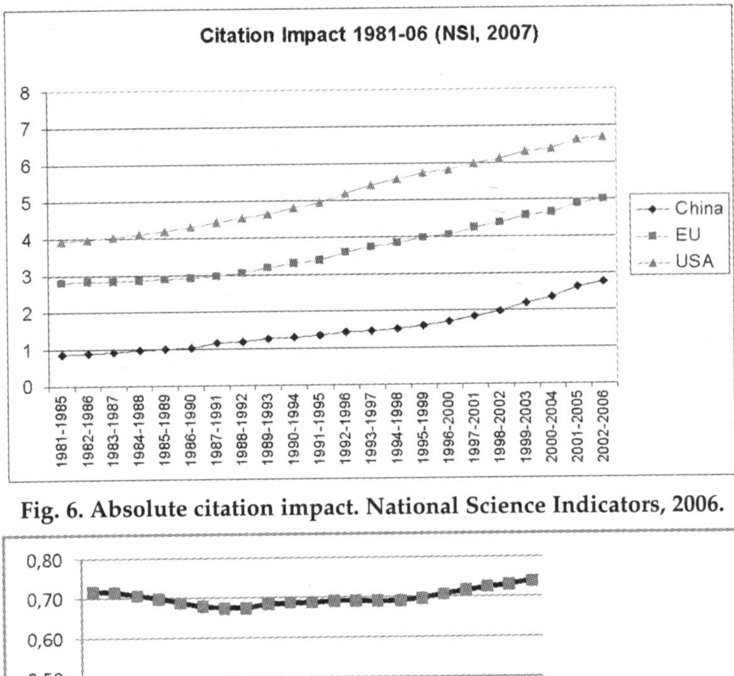

Fig. 6. Absolute citation impact. National Science Indicators, 2006.

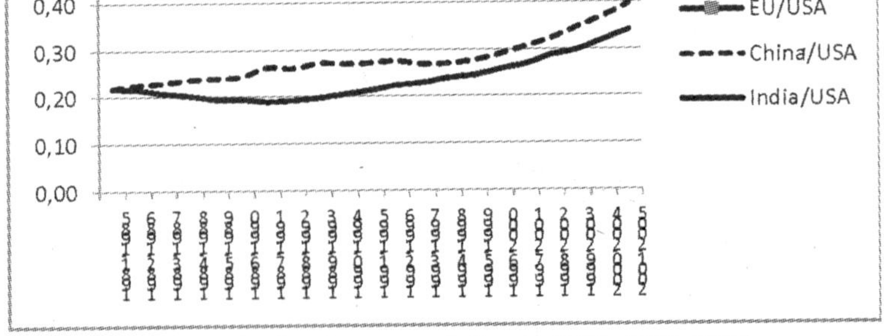

Fig. 7. Citation impact relative to USA. NSI, 2006.

The citation impacts are growing in parallel for the three entities, but as demonstrated by the diagram, Fig. 7, China and India are in parallel diminishing the impact gap to EU and USA according to Web of Science data, relatively speaking. One reason may very well be that for China and India the *citedness* ratios increased from 27 % to 52 % and 34 % to 49 %, respectively, during the twenty-five year period.

CROWN INDICATORS

Crown Indicators (van Raan, 1999; Moed, 2005) are relative impact indicators for a given entity that are *normalized* in relation to the entity research field(s) globally. Two different Crown Indicators are in operation, both producing index number(s) as indicator result:

1. Journal Crown Indicator – JCI : the ratio between the *real number of citations* received by a given unit during a given period (diachronic analysis) and the diachronic citation *impact of the corresponding journals* used by the unit during the same period – the *expected impact*. The set of journals defines the exact research profile for which the unit makes research;

2. Field Crown Indicator – FCI : the ratio between the *real number of citations* received by a given unit during a given period (diachronic analysis) and the global diachronic *citation impact weighted according to the research profile* (in terms of fields) displayed by the unit during the same period: $\Sigma c/\Sigma(C/P_{field} \times p_{field})$ – where c is the citations received by the unit, C/P_{field} signifies the global citation impact of a research field of the unit's research profile and p_{field} the number of publications produced in that field by the unit.

In serious research evaluations one would never apply the synchronous JIF mentioned above, mainly because it signifies the average citation impact of the articles in a journal for a very short period (1-2 years), and partly because the JIF is only with difficulty comparable with other real citation values.

India, Research Profile 2001-05		India c/p	Cits.	Publ.	Profile	Global C/P	Field Crown Indicator	Shadow country Weighted Cits.
Agricultural & Plant Sc.	2001-2005	0.99	12941	13050	11.9	2.89	0.34	37763
Biology & Biochemistry	2001-2005	3.1	17469	5636	5.2	7.56	0.41	42625
Chemistry	2001-2005	2.78	70220	25228	23.2	4.28	0.65	107858
Clinical Medicine	2001-2005	2.28	23093	10123	9.3	5.40	0.42	54651
Computer Science	2001-2005	1.06	831	783	0.7	1.51	0.71	1178
Ecology/Environment	2001-2005	1.67	4400	2627	2.4	3.59	0.47	9444
Engineering	2001-2005	1.19	10405	8724	8.0	1.78	0.67	15532
Geosciences	2001-2005	1.76	5427	3081	2.8	3.40	0.51	10592
Immunology	2001-2005	3.69	2438	660	0.6	10.62	0.35	7009
Materials Science	2001-2005	1.86	14387	7724	7.1	2.54	0.73	19597
Mathematics	2001-2005	0.74	1064	1438	1.3	1.32	0.56	1905
Microbiology	2001-2005	3.26	5751	1764	1.6	6.90	0.47	12164
Molecular Biology & Genetics	2001-2005	4.73	5738	1214	1.1	12.63	0.37	15336
Multidisciplinary	2001-2005	1.36	4621	3404	3.1	4.48	0.30	15252
Neurosciences & Behavior	2001-2005	4.01	3132	782	0.7	7.88	0.51	6166
Pharmacology	2001-2005	2.51	6476	2583	2.4	5.01	0.50	12935
Physics & Space Sc.	2001-2005	3.02	57849	19132	17.6	4.12	0.73	78886
Social Sciences, general	2001-2005	0.9	846	940	0.9	1.99	0.45	1875
Ratio of Sums		2.27	247088	108893	100	4,69	0.48	450768

(Weighted) Field Crown Indicator: 247,088 / 450,767.59 = ***0.55***

Fig. 8. Indian research profile of 18 fields with global field citation impacts and the weighted expected Indian citations according to number of publications. Gray areas are most research rich fields. NSI, 2006.

Fig. 8 illustrates the comprehensive FCI calculation table for a country. To the left the column outlines the 18 research fields constituting the Indian profile, 2001-2005. Next are the corresponding national field impact factors (c/p), the number of citations and publications per field, and the research profile given in percent of the total research output. We observe that in India three fields stand out: Chemistry (23.2 %); Physics and Space Sciences (17.6 %); and Agriculture and Plant Sciences (11.9 %). Also Engineering is a research rich field (8 %).

The Global field impact (C/P per field) is followed by the corresponding FCI per field for India, with Physics and Space Sciences having the highest FCI (.73). The last column named "Shadow country, weighted Cits." demonstrates the result of the calculation of the *expected* number of citations India should have had per field, given the Indian number of publications per field multiplied by the Global field impact. As an example, in Agriculture and Plant Sciences the *actual* number of citations received by India is 12,941, but according to the number of publications (13,050) and the Global impact (2.89) India should have *expected* to obtain (13,050 x 2.89) = 37,763 citations. All the (weighted) expected citations are then summed up and divided into the sum of the actual citations received across all the fields in the Indian research profile (247,088/450,768), providing the overall FCI for India, 2001-2005, lower right-hand corner: index value *.55*.

This correct way of calculation is called *'ratio of sums'* between the *weighted* sum of citations and the sum of actually received citations by the unit. It serves as a kind of global 'shadow' or 'mirror unit' so that the comparison is done conditioned by the actual research profile of the unit – not any other profile.

One commonly used quick and dirty way of doing the calculation is simply to divide the unit's overall real impact (India: 2.27) by the global impact (previously calculated as 'ratio of sums': 4.69) providing an impact index value of *.48*. However, this calculation effectively compares India with the predominant global actor: USA! Another way is to divide the real Indian impact (2.27) by the 'sum of ratios', i.e., the sum of all the global field impacts divided by the number of fields (= 4.88 – not shown on diagram). This implies to regard all fields having *equal research importance*, which is clearly not the Indian case. The resulting (false) relative impact index value = *.47*. The only fair comparison is the first mode of calculation demonstrated above.

This is also demonstrated quite forcefully by Fig. 9. In China's case we observe that their research profile is different from that of India (and that of Denmark, Fig. 10): Agriculture and Plant sciences do not play an important role. Although the Global citation impact per field is the same as for India, Fig. 8, the 'weighted cits.' column display quite different amounts of expected citations for China compared to India. This is owing to the different research profile and the different number of publications in the fields between the two countries. Finally, we again observe that the *overall FCI* for China (.67) is higher than the crude USA-dominated calculation (.56). This is because the Chinese research profile, like that of India, is very different from the global USA dominated profile. Comparing India and China we observe that only in Physics and Space Sciences does India display a higher FCI (.73 vs. .62).

China, Research Profile 2001-05		China c/p	Cits	Publ.	*Profile %*	Global C/P	Field Crown Indicator	Shadow Country Weighted Cits.
Agricultural & Plant Sc.	2001-2005	2.19	21137	9653	4.18	2.89	0.76	27897.17
Biology & Biochemistry	2001-2005	3.66	30563	8352	3.62	7.56	0.48	63141.12
Chemistry	2001-2005	2.89	155384	53851	23.34	4.28	0.68	230482.28
Clinical Medicine	2001-2005	4.28	75917	17736	7.69	5.4	0.79	95774.4
Computer Science	2001-2005	1.17	3821	3256	1.41	1.51	0.77	4916.56
Ecology/Environment	2001-2005	2.26	10907	4835	2.10	3.59	0.63	17357.65
Engineering	2001-2005	1.47	35873	24463	10.60	1.78	0.83	43544.14
Geosciences	2001-2005	2.54	19422	7655	3.32	3.44	0.74	26333.2
Immunology	2001-2005	4.33	3976	918	0.40	10.62	0.41	9749.16
Materials Science	2001-2005	2.07	40779	19684	8.53	2.54	0.81	49997.36
Mathematics	2001-2005	1.1	8542	7732	3.35	1.32	0.83	10206.24
Microbiology	2001-2005	4.19	10027	2394	1.04	6.9	0.61	16518.6
Molecular Biology & Genetics	2001-2005	7.26	18395	2533	1.10	12.63	0.57	31991.79
Multidisciplinary	2001-2005	2.24	14650	6531	2.83	4.48	0.50	29258.88
Neurosciences & Behavior	2001-2005	4.37	10384	2374	1.03	7.88	0.55	18707.12
Pharmacology	2001-2005	2.47	8963	3633	1.57	5.01	0.49	18201.33
Physics & Space Sc.	2001-2005	2.56	138329	53109	23.02	4.12	0.62	218809.08
Social Sciences general	2001-2005	1.65	3245	1971	0.85	1.99	0.83	3922.29
Ratio / Sum		2.65	610,314	230,680	100	4.69	*0.56*	916,808
		(Weighted) Field Crown Indicator: (610,314 / 916,808.37 =						***0.67***

Fig. 9. Research profile of the 18 fields of China 2001-2005. Legend as in Fig. 9. NSI, 2006.

Fig. 10 show a typical case for a small West-European country, Denmark. The research profile is very different from those of India and China, with a very heavy focus on Clinical Medicine (26.2 %) and less on Agriculture and Plant Sciences (11.3 %), Biology (11 %) and Physics and Space Sciences (10 %).

We observe that in contrast to India and China the overall FCI for Denmark is *lower* than the crude calculation (1.31 vs. 1.41). This is because too many publications in high-impact fields like Immunology and Neuroscience are not receiving sufficient number of citations. The expected (weighted) number of citations in those fields is having greater influence on the overall Danish FCI (c/C*) than does the un-weighted Global FCI (4.65) - hence the extensive difference between 1.41 and 1.31. The same loss happens for other North European countries like Finland (Ingwersen et al, ISSI 2007).

Denmark, Research Profile, 2001-2005				Publ.		*FCI per field:*	Shadow Country
Field	Citations = c	Publ.	DK-c/p	Share %	Global C/P	c/p / C/P	*Weighted C**
Agriculture & Plant Sc.	21.393	5.202	4,11	*11,33*	2,89	***1,42***	15053,05
Biology & Biochemistry	43.066	5.063	8,51	*11,02*	7,56	***1,12***	38291,09
Chemistry	25.432	3.959	6,42	*8,62*	4,28	***1,50***	16925,96
Clinical Medicine	93.635	12.033	7,78	*26,20*	5,27	***1,48***	63439,93
Computer Science	771	362	2,13	*0,79*	1,51	***1,42***	544,84
Ecology/Environment	8.440	1.826	4,62	*3,98*	3,59	***1,29***	6564,28
Economics & Business	1.099	712	1,54	*1,55*	1,82	***0,85***	1295,88
Engineering	5.784	2.180	2,65	*4,75*	1,78	***1,49***	3881,32
Geosciences	7.770	1.559	4,98	*3,39*	3,44	***1,45***	5359,84
Immunology	8.774	992	8,84	*2,16*	10,62	***0,83***	10535,10
Materials Science	1.897	576	3,29	*1,25*	2,54	***1,30***	1461,37
Mathematics	996	540	1,84	*1,18*	1,32	***1,39***	715,23
Microbiology	12.586	1.495	8,42	*3,25*	6,90	***1,22***	10309,15
Molecular Biology & Genetics	17.919	1.217	14,72	*2,65*	12,63	***1,17***	15374,36
Multdisciplinary	2.626	532	4,94	*1,16*	4,48	***1,10***	2383,70
Neuro Sc.& Behavior	11.470	1.560	7,35	*3,40*	7,88	***0,93***	12300,02
Pharmacology	5.442	975	5,58	*2,12*	5,01	***1,11***	4882,39
Physics & Space Sc.	30.483	4.574	6,66	*9,96*	4,12	***1,62***	18859,64
Social Sc. general	1.133	573	1,98	*1,25*	1,50	***1,32***	860,18
Sum:	300.716	45.930	***6,55***	*100,00*	*4,65*	1,41	229037,32
WEIGHTED C* = C/P * p (per field)				**FCIm = Ratio c / C* =**			***1,31***

Fig. 10. Research profile of the 18 fields of Denmark 2001-2005. Gray-shaded areas in FCI column are high-impact fields; boxed cells signify low-impact. NSI, 2006.

To sum up one should note that the more fair one wishes to carry out the research evaluation of a unit compared to other units the more complex the calculations become. Similarly, the interpretations of the results become increasingly complex and involve more factors than observed on the surface. Hence the necessity to involve domain experts in the process.

PUBLICATION POINT SYSTEMS - THE NORDIC MODEL

The citation impact calculations discussed above demonstrate that they are functional for the sciences and some selected social sciences, namely the ones that are 'science-like', such as Political Science, Organizational Science and Public Administration, Economics and Business, Library and Information Science, either because they are rather empirical and/or international in nature or because their principal publication vehicles are journal articles and conference papers.

However, the other social sciences, like Sociology, and the fields of the humanities are difficult to handle outside the English-dominated countries. This owes to their local or regional scopes and their publication patterns, e.g., mainly in the form of monographs and writing in the local language. The observation of citations from and to monographs has always posed problems for Informetrics. The citation indexes are only lately increasingly incorporating German, Spanish and French journals, conference proceedings *and* monographs, like in Scopus and Google Scholar/Books. In addition, the blind-folded peer reviewing process known from the sciences and some social sciences is thus far scarcely applied in the humanities.

In order to circumvent this unbalanced situation the Norwegian government, and later the Danish one, decided to apply 'publication points' as a measure for the distribution of public research funding to their universities. For the Danish public research budget 2011 the following weighted allocation model is used (weights in %):

- Ph.D. degrees: 5 %;
- Number of students: 45 %;
- External funding: 35 %;
- The 'bibliometric indicator': 15 %.

In 2012-13 the weight of the so-called 'bibliometric indicator', based on the publication points, increases to 25 %, taken from the student and external funding factors. The indicator works in the following way for *all* publication types that are *peer reviewed* across all academic fields, including the humanities (Schneider 2009).

Sixty eight (68) academic field committees were established in 2007-08, each constituted by appointed field experts from the various universities, thus covering the entire spectrum of academia. Each committee selected the range of *peer reviewed* journals, conferences and monographic publishers applying peer review, pertaining to their field. A journal can only be placed in one field according to the system. They were supported by a dedicated journal database system with an interface to add, delete or edit ISSN and journal titles from the lists. Conferences and publishers were added manually by the experts according to field. Only international and national journals can be selected. Local institutional journals or series are only qualified if more than half of the contents is from outside the institution - it is then seen as a 'national' vehicle.

This resulted in a comprehensive list of approximately 19,000 journals. The equivalent list for Norway made a year earlier was only covering 16,000 journals. This list is divided into two levels: *Level 2* journals (and monographic publishers), which are constituted by the core high-quality journals covering maximum 1/5 of the publications worldwide in that field. They are identified through peer consensus in each committee. The idea is to push scientists to publish in these Level 2 journals. The remaining journals (publishers) constitute *Level 1*. An article from Level 2 obtains 3 points while a Level 1 item gets 1 point; conference papers obtain .7 points and a Level 2 monograph receives 8 points. 5 points are given to Level 1 monographs. Editorial work does not obtain points. (Bi)annual conferences are regarded as journals and high-quality conferences, e.g. in Computer Science, will probably receive higher points than stated here in the future. *Fractional counting* is applied according to the weight of the author affiliations per item. All fractionalized points are summed up per research institution.

The total amount of the Danish publication points based on 2009 publications was 21,950 points allocated 19,900 publications, including patents. The Social Sciences and

Humanities took 3,850 and 3,100 points, respectively, whilst the Sciences and Technology fields and the Health sciences 9,600 and 5,400 points, respectively.

In Norway a centralized database with all Norwegian academic publications *and* their received points is made publicly available. One may here observe and analyze in more depth publication production over periods, institutions, fields and observe behavioral patterns. In Denmark this tool has not yet been achieved. Input is done in a more decentralized way and only the overall point results at institutional and field levels are publicly available on the Web.

The publication points - or the 'bibliometric indicator' - do *not* signify *research quality* but rather publication 'success'! The advantage is that only 'one single' indicator is produced per research entity and that *all academic fields* are included. The disadvantages are several: it is difficult to compare the research output and impact directly between universities or countries by means of the publication points, as done with citation-based indicators, because their research profiles are so different and normalization is cumbersome. Obviously one may observe how many points each university has obtained from the Level 2 journals of their research fields, respectively, and then calculate a top-index value per university - provided that the same point system is used for all the entities. This leads to the publication point indicators described below.

Another disadvantage lies on its misuse: One should not apply the point systems at individual scientist level, since the fractional counting makes teamwork less profitable. The 'bibliometric indicator' would be counterproductive if applied within an institution. Unfortunately, one may foresee that with a high probability, it will be used by individual researchers against each other and by research administrators against individual academics.

PUBLICATION POINT INDICATORS

Along the line of comparing the cumulated points obtained by institutions in their top level journal publications, as suggested above, Elleby and Ingwersen have proposed a Normalized Publication Point Index - nPPI - and other *publication point indicators* (2010). The contribution "[compares] central citation-based indicators with novel publication point indicators (PPIs) that are formalized and exemplified. Two diachronic citation windows are applied: 2006-07 and 2006-08. Web of Science (WoS) as well as Google Scholar (GS) are applied to observe the citation delay and citedness for the different document types published by DIIS, the Danish Institute for International Studies, journal articles, book chapters/conference papers and monographs." (2010, p. 512)

Journal Crown Indicator calculations were based on WoS. Three PPIs were proposed by Elleby and Ingwersen: the Publication Point Ratio (PPR), which measures the sum of obtained publication points over the sum of the ideal points for the same set of documents; the Cumulated Publication Point Indicator (CPPI), which graphically illustrates the *cumulated gain* of actually obtained vs. ideal points, both seen as vectors for the same publication types; and the normalized Cumulated Publication Point Index (nCPPI) that represents the cumulated gain of publication success as index values, either graphically or as one overall score for the institution under evaluation (Järvelin and Kekäläinen, 2002; Järvelin and Persson, 2008).

As stated by Elleby and Ingwersen, (p. 512), "[the] case study indicates that for smaller interdisciplinary research institutions the citation delay is substantial (2-3 years to obtain a citedness of 50 %) when applying WoS for articles. Applying GS implies a shorter delay and much higher citedness for all document types. Statistical significant correlations were only found between WoS and GS and the two publication point systems in between[1*], respectively. The study demonstrates how the nCPPI can be applied to institutions as evaluation tools supplementary to JCI in various combinations, in particular when institutions include humanistic and social science disciplines."

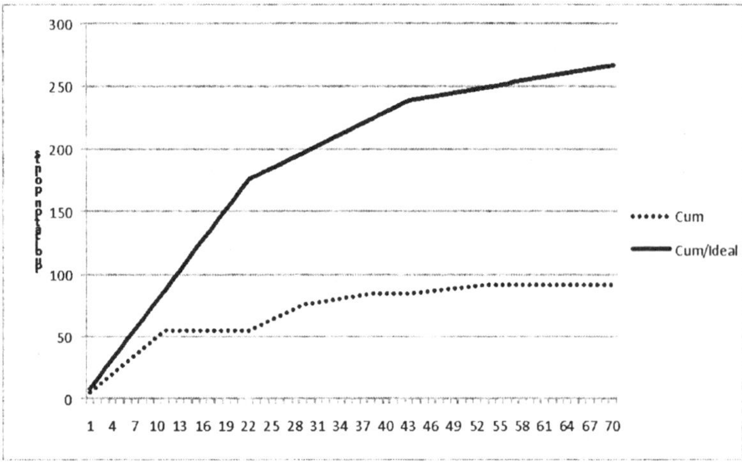

Fig. 11. Cumulated gain vectors for the actually obtained fractionalized publication points by DIIS 2006 (n = 71) and the ideal vector for the same DIIS publications.

Comparisons between institutions applying the publication points can thus be carried out within specific ranges of publication vector values through their normalized CPPI. Figures 11 and 12 demonstrate the principle by displaying cumulated actual vectors versus expected (ideal) ones (Fig. 11) and the corresponding normalization curve for DIIS publications 2006 (Fig. 12).

The ideal value, Fig. 12, is index value 1 and we observe how the point-heavy monographs initially obtain a score of .63 for then to drop to .3. The increase (from doc. no. 22) results from an improvement of gain among some journal articles later to flatten since the two vector curves, Fig. 11, starts to run more in parallel.

* [1] Between Norwegian/Danish system and a local DIIS publication point system.

The DIIS data illustrate the various ways to apply the PPIs combined with citation scores. "[DIIS] would have received funding in 2008 according to 129.2 Norwegian publication points received 2006 for its 71 peer-reviewed publications. That sum [would] release research funding of X amount. The overall nCPPI for DIIS 2006 was .41. The rules for neutral funding might (as an illustration) be set to a nCPPI index value of .50, signifying a publication success gain of 50 %. If below .50 the funding of X would be reduced; if above .50 it would be increased.

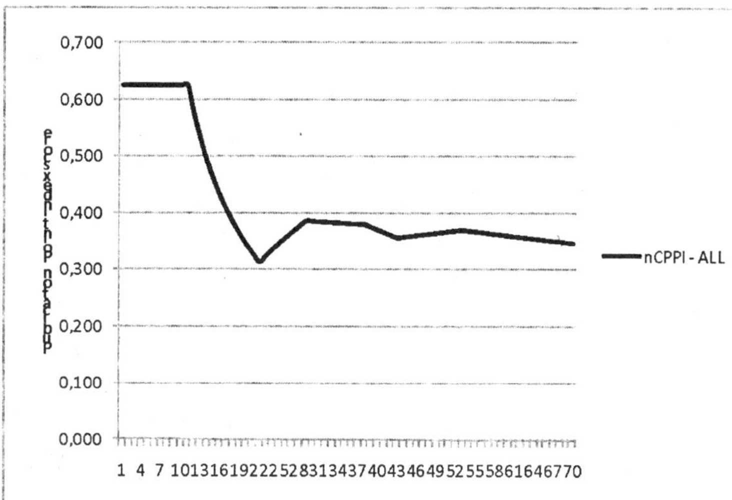

Fig. 12. Normalized Cumulated Publication Point vector for DIIS 2006 (n= 71).

In 2009 the calculation of the JCI$^{2006\text{-}08}$ could take place for the DIIS articles published 2006 – a three year citation window. It shows an index value of 1.4, i.e., a value above the *expected* world average for the same journals. One might hence re-adjust the ensuing funding by a factor owing to this positive demonstration of social (world-wide) scientific *citation impact* of the published research two years earlier." (2010, p. 521-522).

The nCPPI score can hence be combined with the corresponding JCI score for the same journal articles, into an *integrated* score: $\gamma^n = JCI^n \times nCPPIn^n$ - for *n* documents. If DIIS is used as an illustration the 22 articles (*n*) received a JCI index score for 2006-08 at 1.4. The same *n* documents obtained a nCPPI score at .66.

As stated in Elleby and Ingwersen (2010, p.521-522), "[the] exemplified γ^n-score *.92* signifies that the DIIS impact of the articles has been reduced to below 1.0 (the world impact) because the cumulated publication gain for the same articles was too small. Thus, there exists a trade-off between the nCPPI score (0 – 1.0) and the JCI (≥ 0) value. A low nCPPI score implies that too few journals applied by the unit belonged to the higher level of the Publication Point system. With a low nCPPI score the JCI value must be very high to compensate if the final score should stay at world average. With a large cumulated gain of publication success points, e.g. a nCPPI score at .80 (signifying that 80 % of the ideal gain has been obtained), the JCI for DIIS could be less (e.g. 1.25) to reach the integrated γ^n-score = 1.0. When nCPPI is high it means that the major portion of the articles was published in high-level journals obtaining the maximum (ideal) amount of points available according to the publication point system. If the γ^n-score in that case is below 1.0 that implies that the institution had great difficulty in achieving the expected (high) world citation impact. Thus, the nCPPI works similar to a Field Crown Indicator (van Raan, 1999) which, when compared to the corresponding JCI, shows the true impact level of the journals used.

There is indeed space for additional publication point indicators. For instance, one may apply different document cutoff positions (*i*) over long document lists from large institutions, e.g. i^{100}; i^{200}; ... i^n, in order to compare the cumulated publication success gain at the start of the accumulation, where the index values supposedly are 1 or close to one, and later across comparable institutions.

CONCLUSION

With open access we can foresee a nightmare as concerns tracking qualified and authoritative scientific publications, aside from the application of the citation indexes. This situation arises from the lack of bibliographic control of what is original vs. parallel and spin-off versions and simply opinionated documents over *many* institutional repositories - and re-mixed on the web with all other document types incl. blog entries and other Web 2.0 manifestations.

The peer reviewed publications are the main ones to analyze - also when applying different kinds of citation-based indicators, Crown Indicators or *h*-indexes. Publication Point Indicators are indeed more current than citations, mirroring last year's productivity. But they solely state something about publication success, not the quality of the contents. However, as shown in this lecture Publication Point Indicators can be combined with citation-based indicators, e.g., the Journal Crown Indicator for corresponding sets of journal articles. This integrated γ^n-score may be used to compare across institutions and other entities given that the same publication point system is used across the units. For other document types than articles the nCPPI indicator may work as a supplement to the γ^n-score.

The principle of comparing the real publication point cumulated score with the ideal one for the same documents derives from systems evaluation methods developed in Information Retrieval research (Järvelin and Kekäläinen, 2002; Järvelin and Persson, 2008). With this knowledge transfer across these two information science fields we observe once again how they benefit from one another.

2

The Range of Webometrics : Forms of Digital Social Utility As Tools

Initially, this lecture places Webometrics in the broader context of Informetrics, Scientometrics, Cybermetrics and Bibliometrics. Link structures and levels of importance for Webometric analyses are outlined. We then proceed with an overview of the potentials of Webometrics, ranging from search engine and link analyses, including a discussion of the Web Impact Factor (WIF) and the technical but false citation-link association, over trend analysis using social utility tools such as blogs, to a discussion of new scientific Dataset Usage Indicators. The lecture ends with concluding remarks.

THE CONTEXT OF WEBOMETRICS

According to Björneborn and Ingwersen (2001; 2004) Webometrics is concerned with the study of quantitative aspects of the construction and use of information resources, structures and technologies on the Web, drawing on bibliometric and informetric methods:

- Search engine performance
- Link structures, e.g., Web Impact Factors, cohesiveness of link topologies, etc.
- Users' information behaviour (searching, browsing, etc.)
- Web page contents - knowledge mining - blog trends
- Dataset analyses and impact

Webometrics is narrower in scope than *Cybermetrics* that signify quantitative studies of the whole Internet, not only the Web - see Fig. 1 - i.e., chat, mailing lists, news groups, MUDs, etc.

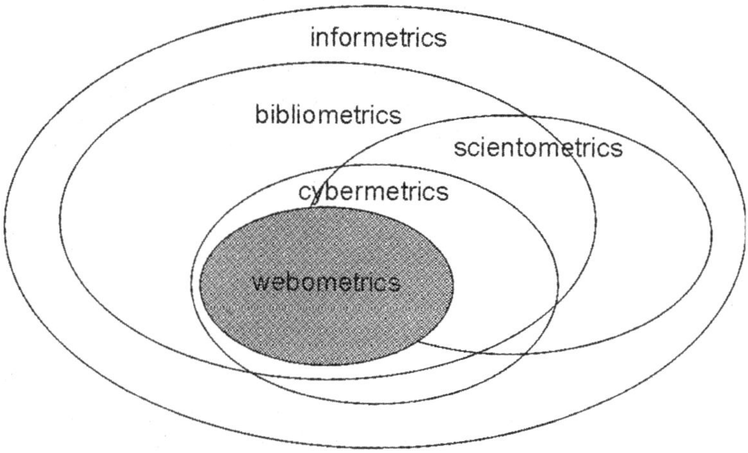

Fig. 1. The Informetric landscape; from Björneborn and Ingwersen (2001).

Informetrics circumscribes the other metrics, so that all *Bibliometric* methods and tools are included. Some *Scientometric* analyses may deal with, for instance, health science statistics, such as number of beds or doctors/nurses, which are not Bibliometrics proper. Some scientometric analyses may be conducted on the Internet (Aguilo, 1998) (*Cybermetrics*), e.g. e-mail analyses among scientists, and some may involve academic sources on the Web. *Webometrics*, originally coined as a concept by Almind and Ingwersen (1997), forms part of Bibliometrics and Cybermetrics. However, some Webometric analyses may deal with non-scientific information, such as daily-life blogs, and other social media analyses, search engine coverage for informetric analysis in general, etc.

The most important characteristic of Webometrics is the application of *link structures* when carrying out a variety of measurements. Fig. 2 illustrates this variety of link types, wherein particular transversal links may lead to 'small world' phenomena (Adamic; Björneborn; Granovetter).

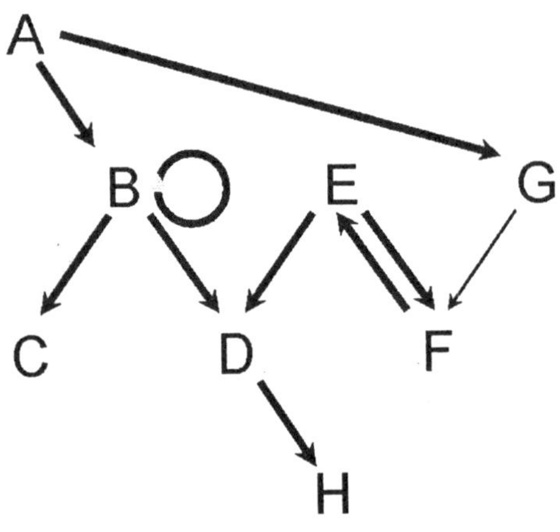

Fig. 2. Link terminology – basic concepts; from Björneborn and Ingwersen (2001).

The concepts, Fig. 2, are explained as follows. *B* has an *outlink* to C; outlinking corresponds to, but is not the same as referencing. *B* has an *inlink* from A; to obtain an inlink corresponds to, but is not the same as receiving a citation. *B* has a *selflink*; selflinking corresponds to, but is not the same as a self-citation.

A has *no inlinks*; to be non-linked corresponds to, but is not the same as being non-cited. *E* and *F* are *reciprocally* linked. *A* is *transitively* linked with *H* via *B* and *D*. H is reachable from *A* by a directed *link path. A* has a *transversal link* to G, i.e. a *short cut.*

C and *D* are *co-linked* from B, i.e., they have *co-inlinks* or *shared inlinks,* which corresponds to, but is not the same as co-citation. *B* and *E* are *co-linking* to *D*, i.e., they have *co-out-links* or *shared outlinks,* which corresponds to, but is not the same as bibliographic coupling.

The association between linking and referencing-citations is discussed below in connection to the WIF. However, it is vital that the superficial technical similarity does not confuse people in believing that they are the same. But obviously, the same mathematical treatments can be done on co-linking phenomena as on co-citation and bibliographic coupling. That is because both linking and references-citations fundamentally are directed graphs (Broder). Both Björneborn (2001) and Kleinberg and Lawrence (2001) have discussed the nature and structure of the Web, among others.

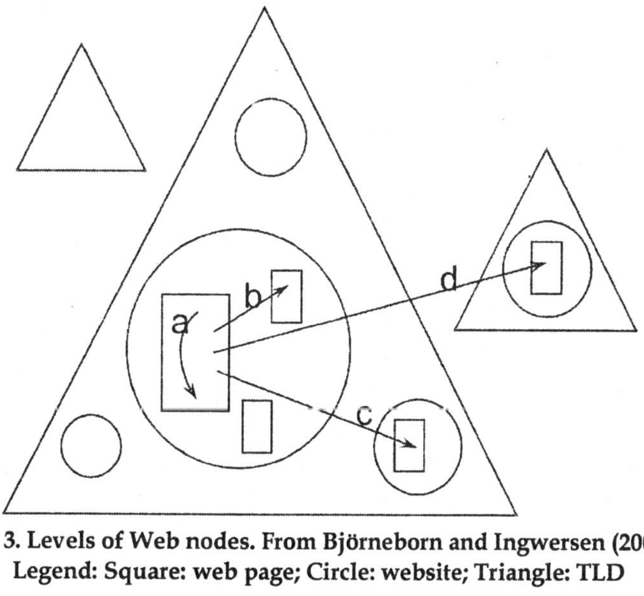

Fig. 3. Levels of Web nodes. From Björneborn and Ingwersen (2001). Legend: Square: web page; Circle: website; Triangle: TLD

In the academic world we have articles or conference papers published in journals and/or conference proceedings. We also have individual works published in anthologies. One might argue that a digitized institutional repository actually contains the former levels of publication, serving as a meta-channel of publication. We observe here a three-level hierarchy of works and publications: repository; journal/proceedings; work or article/paper. However, on the Web there may indeed exist more levels - like Russian dolls. Fundamentally however, we deal with three levels of nodes and links, Fig. 3.

On the figure we observe three TLDs (Top level Domains) as triangles. The large one may, for instance, illustrate a country, like .dk. Inside the TLD four circles illustrate four different Websites, each holding one or several Web pages. Accordingly, a Web page may contain selflinks (a), page outlinks *also seen as* site selflinks (b), site outlinks *also seen as* TLD selflinks (c), and TLD outlinks (d). It is consequently obvious that during web link analyses one must be very careful to control *the level* at which the analyses are carried out.

SEARCH ENGINE ANALYSIS

Bar-Ilan is one of the most productive researchers in search engine analysis and methodology, including longitudinal studies (1997; 2004). Also the Thelwall groups have contributed many substantial analyses on the matter, see for instance (Thelwall, 2000; Kousha and Thelwall, 2007; ARIST). One aspect of search engine analysis is their growth in volume and the distribution over different engines, as well as their coverage. Secondly, the overlap of Webometrics with Scientometrics, Fig. 1, constitutes an important aspect for analysis: how much scientific sources does the web contain, and with which characteristics?

The first aspect, growth and coverage, is quite difficult to assess because one cannot trust the number of 'hits' provided by the search engines during searching. Secondly, local analyses are very cumbersome to carry out since only a small fraction of the retrieved Web sources can be viewed or downloaded. Each engine has its limitations, e.g. Google makes available the 800 most highly ranked units retrieved; other engines allow less or a bit more. Fig. 4 demonstrates a distribution of number of searches in USA, their growth and shares per engine in August, 2009. The Website Internetworldstats.com provides general Internet and Web statistics, with some time delay.

Top 10 Search Providers for August 2009, Ranked by Searches (U.S.)

Search Provider	Searches (000)	Month-on-Month Growth (%)	Share of Searches (%)
Total	**10,812,734**	2.9	100
Google	6,986,580	2.6	64.6
Yahoo	1,726,060	-4.2	16
MSN/Windows Live/Bing	1,156,415	22.1	10.7
AOL	333,231	1.8	3.1
Ask.com	186,270	2.9	1.7
My Web	128,432	0.5	1.2
Comcast	50,328	-21.6	0.5
Yellow Pages	37,923	2.7	0.4
NexTag	31,830	0.4	0.3
Local.com	16,314	2.9	0.2

Source: NielsenMegaView Search

Fig. 4. Number of searches on Web search engines in USA, August 2009, their growth and shares in %. Source: http:// searchenginewatch.com

The second aspect, the volume of scientific sources on the Web, was first dealt with simultaneously by Lawrence and Giles (1999) and Allen et al. (1999). The former estimated that approximately 6 % of the Web is academic in nature. The latter team investigated how biological topics was dealt with on the Web. They found that 46 % of their sample of 500 Webpages was 'informative' on the topic; 54 % was not. Of the 'informative' ones 10-35 % was 'inaccurate' and 20-35 % 'misleading' - depending on the topic. Only 52 % of the 'informative' webpages contained academic references. Almost the same pattern was found in a later study by Jepsen et al. (2004), covering several engines.

While it would seem alright to apply the web search engines for this kind of *data capture* and analysis, since one operates with sampling and not complete populations, some problems exist that concern *all kinds* of Webometric research: (1) the dependency of each search engine's own *ranking algorithm* in terms of the output, which forms the basis for analysis; (2) the aforementioned limitation as to download of retrieved web items; (3) the scarcity of search engines providing link analysis features. The latter issue is grave since at present only the Yahoo Site Explorer (Yahoo) provides such command features. Otherwise, analyses may only be done through the application of a Web Crawler.

WEB IMPACT FACTOR

It was originally proposed by Ingwersen (1998) – at the same time as Kleinberg (1998) suggested his hubs and authority page-based Web retrieval algorithm, which was close to the PageRank algorithm for Google (Brin and Page, 1998) also proposed the same year. All three ideas were based on the pretext or assumption that links worked 'like' academic references (outlinks) and citations (inlinks). After much research we now know that this 'similarity' is only technical and indeed superficial, and that links and references

/ citations are *not* of the same kind - see below for further discussion.

There are several kinds of Web Impact Factors that may be calculated, provided that a data capture mechanism exists:

- *E-journal Web-IF* - calculated by
  - Inlinks;
  - Citations (as traditional JIF);
- *Academic web site - IF* (calculated by link analyses)
  - National - regional (some URL-problems in TDL exist)
  - Institutions - single sites
  - Other entities, e.g. Web domains
- *Other site types - WIF*, e.g. commercial sites
- *Blog IF*: number of external inlinks to blog / blog entries
- *Twitter IF*: number of external inlinks / twitter entries (Holmberg, 2009)

For e-journals (and blogs or Twitter, etc.) one may analyze the number of inlinks to articles in specific e-journals - like one would do applying citations to the same entities. This indicator will be quite robust because in contrast to 'Web pages' e-journal articles are easy to define and count. Academic WIF and other types of Web-based impact factors suffer from the data capture issue mentioned above. In addition, many TLDs act across the national domains. When collection 'all' .dk Websites in an engine (this is not possible in the sense of downloading all the pages, only to observe the number of hits) there will still be Danish Websites in other domains, like .com or .EU or .NET. For the academic domain some countries, like USA, UK, Australia, India and China have introduced the notation of .ac or .edu, so that sites are separable from the remaining web. This is not the case in most EU countries, however.

Originally the WIF operated with external, internal and overall WIFs. Early on it became clear to the research community that the problem existed for the denominator: the number of Web pages to be divided into the number of inlinks. At the time of creation (1998) the search engines were quite erratic. However, even when engines are stable in their output the number of pages does not indicate so much. As stated above, the original idea was that web pages were 'like' journal articles and Websites like journals as carriers of information. This analogy is false. As Holmberg (2010, p. 131) put it recently: "[a] document on the web can be a single web page or it can be divided into several web pages, which means that simple web design decisions may have great impact on counting the WIFs." Hence we abandon the Web pages as denominator.

Smith (1999) argued that the external inlinks alone were the most indicative because internal inlinks (selflinks) most often were of navigational nature. Chu, He and Thelwall proposed that inlinks could be regarded as indication of visibility on the Web, whilst outlinks serve as a kind of luminosity (2002). As a matter of fact, inlinks are better indicators of impact on the Web alone or if divided by number of staff in the analyzed unit, e.g. a university (Thelwall, 2002). Alone, the number of inlinks correlates with productivity of a university as measured by number of academic entities (articles, notes, etc.) put on the university website. In hindsight, the staff factor is also quite logical since it is people that create the pages and outlinks *and* use other unit's Web spaces often creating inlinks. Although Thomas and Willett (2000) did not find any significant correlations between number of inlinks (or WIF) and the UK RAE scores for universities, Li et al. (2003) succeeded in observing strong correlations between RAE and a WIF version based on inlinks *divided by* number of staff.

These studies led immediately to the design of two new

Web-based measures: Web Use Factor (WUF) and Web Connectivity Factor (WCF) by Thelwall (2003). WUF implies to use *outlink* counts divided by fulltime staff of the analyzed unit. WUF signifies measure the extent of knowledge import from external Web sources. WCF means to measure the intensity of connectivity between pairs of units, like universities. It is calculated by dividing the number of reciprocal links between the two units by the number of fulltime staff. As stated by Holmberg (2010) both indicators were found to correlate with research productivity at the institutional level.

It is important to stress that not all WIF-like analyses are done on the academic sectors of the Web. Holmberg, for instance, has analyzed the link structures and interlinking properties of municipal websites in Finland (2009). He also tested the use of local populations as the denominator in the calculations.

From the many Webometric analyses concerned with aspects of the WIF and link structures we may observe some general characteristics. Inlinks demonstrate rather *recognition* of the inlinked site and *navigational* functionalities than quality or relevance in an information retrieval sense. A given page-rank algorithm mainly relying on link information in a Web search engine may thus rank at the top the most recognized Websites for a given topical search, not necessarily the most topical relevant sites. To do that common content and query-based retrieval ranking features must be involved, like term weights, semantic distances, etc.

Secondly, it is vital to the research community that retrieval engine facilities like the *Yahoo Site Explorer* exists and are further developed. Without such facilities at engine level the community is limited to individual web crawlers as tools for data capture. This makes reproducibility of analyses very difficult and in-coherent.

Third, the *reasons* for making *outlinks* (which later can be turned into inlinks and counted at the recipient side) have been addressed and compared to making academic references, whereby many differences have been observed between the two kinds of networks. Most links are navigational; some point to authoritative Websites and some sites act as hubs with many outlinks (Kelinberg, 1998). But we do more rarely observe normative reasons or conventions for linking, as done associated with scholarly references (and citations). We do not add negative links to a Webpage.

However, some *additional reasons* for linking may overlap reasons for scholarly referencing: Emphasis of own point of perspective, position or relationship; sharing knowledge and information for various purposes; acknowledgements; drawing attention of external information. One should also note the issues of *time* that often are somewhat different from those associated with scholarly communication. As Glänzel has put it: *aging* of sources are different on the Web. You can have birth, maturity and obsolescence happening like in the academic world, but very much faster on the Web. Decline and death of sources and Websites may likewise occur, but marriage; divorce; remarriage; face-lifting; death and resurrection - and alike liberal phenomena are found on the web - rarely on the academic publication scene.

SOCIAL UTILITY INDICATORS

Social utility indicators are metrics that apply Web 2.0 log information on users' searching, downloading, blogging, etc. behavior in order to measure various aspects of the *use* of Web sources. In this final sub-section we exemplify two different kinds of indicators: one dealing with the use of scientific datasets through searches and downloads; and one metric concerned with blogs through the Nielsen Blog Pulse.

BIODIVERSITY DATASET USAGE INDICATORS

In scientific communication *scientific datasets* are often vital to the articles presenting empirical results, e.g. in physics, bio-chemistry and biology. However, their recognition by means of citations are only indirect, since only the article receives citations - not the underlying datasets. The latter may be created and maintained by researchers different from those doing the experiments and publishing the results in research publications. Consequently, attempts have been made to design improved identification means to and *usage indicators* for scientific datasets, in this case, in the biodiversity science fields.

The Global Biodiversity Information Facility (GBIF), with its main administration located in Copenhagen, Denmark, is an open access web service that hosts a vast proportion of the known biodiversity datasets in the World. These are search and downloadable by means of many different entry points, such as, dataset producer, dataset name, species, etc. Figure 5 displays the structure of the GBIF network. In order to generate dataset usage indicators one has to have access to the GBIF server logs. There are two ways of obtaining that: by application of dedicated processing software available through the GBIF main servers to the scientific community; or by direct access to the logs. The latter is at present only possible for the GBIF staff.

Presently, the indicators exemplified below may be constructed at the GBIF Portal and also to some extent through Aggregator Portals, but not yet at the Project Portal level. According to Chavan and Ingwersen (2010) the idea is to include such levels at a later stage.

According to a new contribution by Ingwersen and Chavan (2011) on the Dataset Usage Indicators (DUI) one may construct bibliometric frequency distributions and usage indicators similar to those applied to research evaluation by means of academic citations. The DUI makes use of the number of *visits* and possible subsequent *downloads* from the dataset providers' datasets. It is thus possible to create *relative* as well as *normalized* weighted indicators. Denmark possesses two different dataset providers available through the GBIF Portal: DanBioInfoFacility (DanBIF) - with 36 datasets; and the HerbariumUA (HUA) provider from University of Aarhus with two datasets.

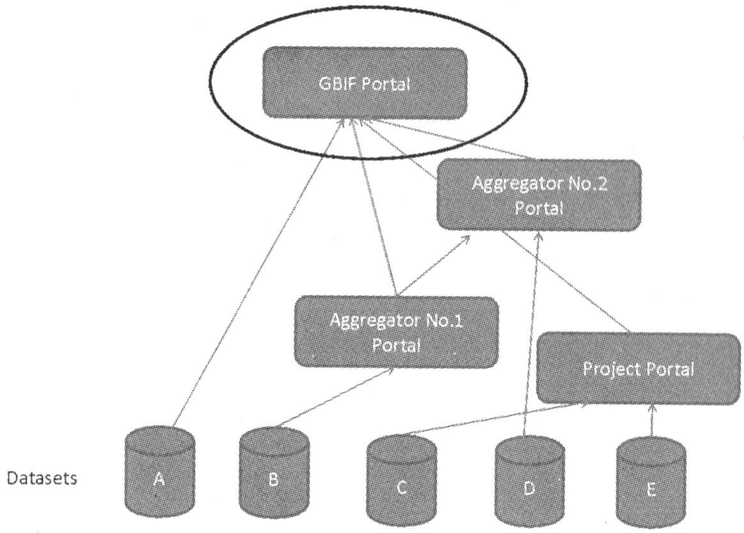

Fig. 5. The GBIF Portal structure (Chavan and Ingwersen, 2010).

GBIF Units	Rec. No. $r(u)$	Download Freq. $d(u)$	Absolute UIF	Relative index UIF to HUA	Relative index UIF to DK
AAU Herbarium dbs.	110,357	716,772	6.50	2.35	20.31
AAU PalmTransect dbs.	148,720	250,330	1.68	0.61	5.25
HUA provider	259,077	717,102	2.77	1.00	8.66
DanBIF, provider	4,995,544	854,761	0.17	-	0.53
Denmark	4,836,771	1,571,863	0.32	-	1.00

Fig. 6. Dataset Usage Impact Factors (UIF) for two datasets and two Danish providers relative to Denmark's UIF. Analysis period: July-December, 2009. GBIF Portal data 31/12, 2009.

As an illustration of DUIs Figure 6 displays the absolute as well as relative usage impact factors for the two Aarhus University datasets, the two Danish dataset providers and Denmark as such. We observe the high absolute and relative UIF for the Herbarium dataset from Aarhus University. The Hua provider and the Danish totals have been cleaned of duplicates. Tests of frequency rank distributions of datasets over providers demonstrate approximations to the Bradford-like distributions known from Bibliometrics, i.e. close to the formula of $a; an; n^2$ (Ingwersen and Chavan, 2011; submitted).

BLOG ANALYSES AND TRENDS

Blogs and other social media manifestations like Twitter, Facebook and LinkDin may also form the basis for usage indicators. Nielsen Blog Pulse provides, for instance, a variety of worldwide trend analyses and indicators. Aside from pre-defined feature trend categories the Nielsen Blog Pulse allows for trend analyses based on user-defined terms, see example, Figure 7. Blog conversations patterns and blog profiles are also available.

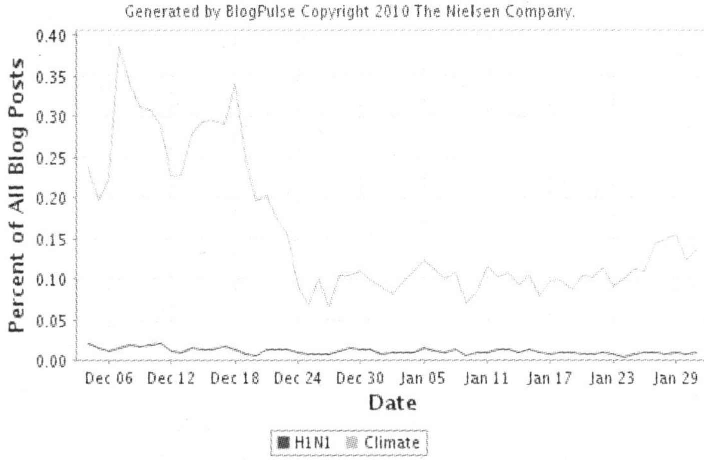

Fig. 7. User-defined blog trend analyses of the 'H1N1 influenza' (lower, dark curve) and the 'climate' discussion around the Copenhagen Summit in December, 2009 (Nielsen Blog Pulse).

Figure 7 demonstrates two user-defined term developments, each representing a concept: the blog entry volume on the H1N1 influenza issue and the more dynamic climate (change) discussion surrounding the Copenhagen Summit meeting. The two peaks represent the start of the Summit and the US president's visit towards its end. We observe how fast the decline in volume takes place after the ending of the meeting December 18, 2009.

CONCLUSIONS

In Webometrics the same methods as in other Informetric analyses are available, although the components may differ. Co-occurrence analyses are indeed possible, both on term and link levels, i.e. co-inlink as well as co-(out)linking (coupling) analyses. Traditional co-citation and bibliographic coupling analyses can be done based on academic citations provided on the Web and compared to the former analyses of the same space.

Bradford-like *frequency rank distributions* are feasible and such distributions may be compared, e.g. in order to observe possible strong ties between high frequency elements or weak ties (small worlds) between low frequency elements of the distributions. Aside from blog analyses Twitter, Facebook and other *social media* may provide foundations for trend analyses, including metrics based on number of 'friends' and other relationships in such networks.

Finally, it is advisable to be cautious concerning the application of the *Web Impact Factor*. WIFs seem better suited when calculated by external inlinks over functional data, such as staff volume or similar non-web-based but relevant features, as denominator. Web impact seems more correlated to the publication volume on the Web of a unit than to its peer assessed quality. Citations as well as inlinks may not necessarily signify relevance from an IR perspective.

On the other hand, information retrieval methodologies are mandatory tools when carrying out informetric analyses including web mining and knowledge discovery (Swanson, 1986). Several bridges link Webometrics/Scientometrics to IR, such as co-occurrence analyses or terms, citations or links and mapping of units (institutions, authors) by means of clustering methods and multi-dimensional scaling. *Web archeology* (Bjorneborn and Ingwersen, 2004) constitutes a retrospective sampling of the past Web structure, as supplied by a range of historical Web archives. Concurrent analyses of the Web may be better off by means of dedicated Web crawlers that carry out structured/stratified sampling of defined Web spaces.

3

Polyrepresentation – Bridging Laboratory Information Retrieval And User Context

This lecture outlines the idea and assumptions underlying the principle of Polyrepresentation, which increasingly can be seen as a theory for Information Retrieval (IR). It points to a variety of empirical studies that support the principle, but that did not rely on it explicitly. This is followed by a discussion of the empirical investigations that directly are founded on Polyrepresentation principles, ideas and assumptions. These investigations deal with polyrepresentation of the information space (documents, databases), retrieval engines (data fusion), the interaction process (relevance feedback, query modification; contextual elements like recommendations), and the cognitive space (user, task and request features).

ORIGIN AND UNDERLYING IDEA AND HYPOTHESIS

Polyrepresentation (or multi-evidence) of documents or searchers was initially mentioned and described by Ingwersen in his monograph "Information Retrieval Interaction" (1992; p. 36; 194-197; 202). A first discussion of the idea underlying the principle was published in an ACM-SIGIR conference paper by Ingwersen in 1994. This was taken forward and put into a comprehensive theoretical discussion based on the cognitive perspective in 1996 as well as on available empirical evidence published through the 1990s.

The underlying idea was based on the cognitive perspective (or viewpoint) of Information Retrieval, which regards all the actors involved in IR as being represented by their interpretations of the IR phenomena (1994; 1996). The cognitive perspective thus talks about how different interpretations of documents (or requests or interaction phenomena) can be made by their authors; human indexers; designers of indexing algorithms; constructors of thesauri/ ontologies; other authors through the network of citations; and searchers, etc. - see illustration Figure 2. Each representation may thus imply an entry point to the item in question, e.g. a document; and an item may be characterized by a multitude of representations.

Polyrepresentation is therefore a direct and *applied consequence* of the integrated cognitive perspective and theory for IR (1996; 2005) by emphasizing the potential benefits in exploiting combinations of (redundant) representations based on their cognitive origins. The underlying hypothesis is:

"The more cognitively or typologically different representations (evidence; features) that point to an information object – and the more intensively they do so – the higher the probability that the object is relevant to the topic, the information need, the situation at hand, or the influencing context of the situation" (2005, p. 208).

Two types of representations are distinctive: *cognitively* different and *functionally* different representations. The former type of representation is associated with interpretations made by different cognitive origins; the latter type is associated with different kinds of representations made by the same origin, see also illustration, Figure 2, e.g. title vs. abstract vs. full text words in an academic publication by the same author(s). The different media are characterized by different sets of cognitive actors and functional representations, as well as different presentation styles that depend on the actual domain, genre and document type. Articles in the humanities are written in a different style from scientific papers, which again are different from news items in magazines or radio/TV broadcasts, etc. One may say that Polyrepresentation is a kind of triangulation of different interpretations of objects. If different interpretations point in the same direction in information space, this implies a higher probability or stronger evidence of relevance.

POLYREPRESENTATION ILLUSTRATED

Why Polyrepresentation in today's information landscape? Polyrepresentation is all about how to exploit different *contexts* and might serve as a common framework for *integrating* various facets of documents, IR engines and interaction as well as searcher characteristics - during the actual retrieval event or over time - see Figure 1. Polyrepresentation is *precision-oriented* in nature, which is a must in a vastly escalating document space, but may also be applied for recall improvement purposes.

If we observe the Document Space (e.g. in scholarly publications) there are several functionally different representations of content in play simultaneously, all under the responsibility of the author(s): Full text terms, following Zipfian distributions; other particular section terms (abstract, introduction, methodology, findings, conclusion); title;

section titles and caption terms; image features; situational assessments of other works in the form of references with their anchor texts (or outlinks with similar anchor texts). Figure 2 illustrates five different groups of cognitive interpretations of academic documents, out of which one concerns the author of documents and its functionally different representations.

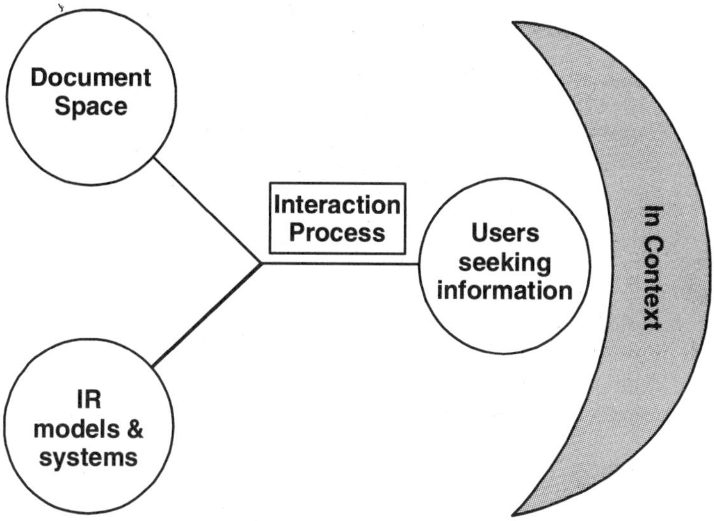

Fig. 1. The central components of Polyrepresentation (based on models from Ingwersen 1992 and 2005).

Indexers (human or algorithmic) make interpretations of the same documents, as does a domain thesaurus constructor and, over time, other authors through their citations (outgoing references and anchor texts turned towards the documents in the inner 'cognitive overlap'). One may envisage a search situation in which request / query terms are found in documents' full text, abstract (author) *but* also as added keywords (human indexer) or/*and* keyword weights (algorithm), *and* through a thesaurus' conceptual structure, *and* further in publication titles or full text *cited by other authors* over time. The Selectors are cognitive actors responsible for the being of the documents, commonly denoted by the metadata of the publications.

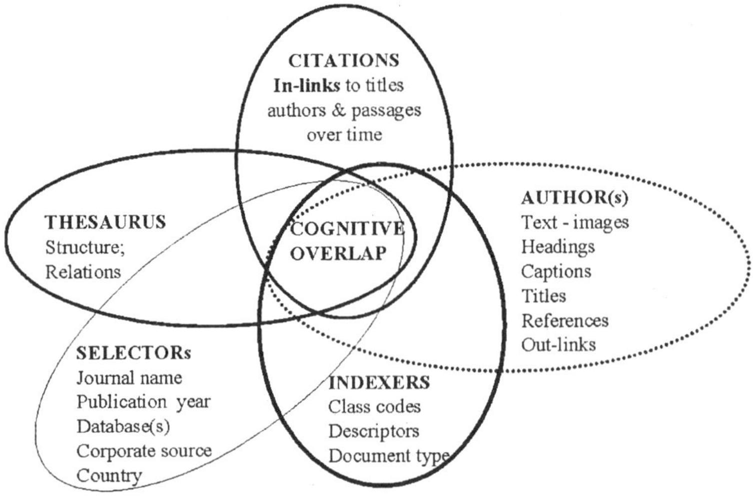

Fig. 2. Polyrepresentation overlaps from five cognitively different representations of scholarly documents, with examples of functionally different representations, based on one searcher statement retrieved from one search engine. (Elaborated from Ingwersen 1996, p. 28 and 2006, p. 149)

Some *social utility* assessments made over time are at play, for instance, the inclusion of documents into journals or conferences is determined by peer reviewing processes; and current author affiliation is a result of employer decisions. The citations (or inlinks) also belong to social utility assessments.

We observe that the *academic references* in the citing documents may serve as a kind of document descriptors (in line with Garfield's original idea behind the citation indexes for retrieval improvements (1979; 1993)). As *citations* they contribute as a temporal access point to the cited documents as well. In addition, the *citation volume* may (or may not) be an useful indicator of importance during retrieval.

The polyrepresentation hypothesis leads to a cognitive

inner overlap of very few (or none) documents. However, the intermediate overlaps may indeed contain documents that satisfy some but not all the cognitively different interpretations that are possible. *Which combinations* of evidence that are the best ones for retrieval should hence be tested empirically.

In an online IR context based on Boolean logic it has always been possible to carry out polyrepresentation. However, it would be quite cumbersome without an algorithmic program. Figure 3 illustrates a very simplistic Boolean command sequence as made in a typical bibliographic database, compared to how it would look in a Polyrepresentation context. To the left-hand side the usual online search command is expressed by searching 'Key A/ TI,DE' in the basic (inverted) index of the database, i.e. searching for search key 'A' among title and descriptor terms simultaneously, and *then* intersected by the journal name (JN=nnnnn). Key 'A' may thus be found in either the title *or* the descriptor field (or in both).

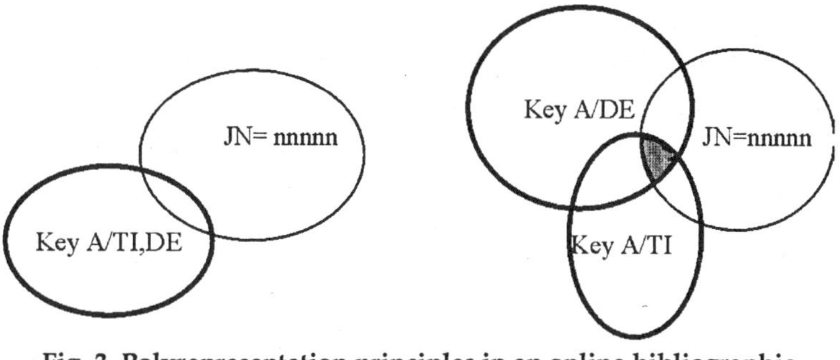

Fig. 3. Polyrepresentation principles in an online bibliographic database context (right) compared to traditional Boolean logic (left). / TI, DE implies that itle and descriptor terms are searched together; JN: journal name. (From 2005, p. 208).

In contrast, the Polyrepresentation hypothesis suggests that the search key 'A' be searched (and hopefully found) in the title field of the inverted index of the database (author representation) *and*, at the same time, be searched (and hopefully found) among the descriptors (indexer representation of document), *and* simultaneously be found in a particular journal (JN=nnnnn). Obviously, the latter logical sequence is more precision-oriented than the former more traditional online (textbook) retrieval method. If a document satisfies the author *and* the indexer simultaneously, by means of identical keys, the hypothesis informs that that document has a higher probability of relevance than documents only satisfying one of the representations. Evidently, a domain ontology may serve as a supporting tool for adding synonyms and closely related keys to the original key 'A' at search time, thus increasing the probability of finding documents dealing with similar conceptual contents that may be relevant in the situation.

"The Polyrepresentation principle may be applied to non-textual information objects of various media types and various genres..." (The Turn, p. 342). For instance, as some students of mine demonstrated a couple of years ago, a graphical object of art can be represented by, e.g. exhibition catalogues, art history books and TV documentaries. It is also evident that Boolean logic is not the only possible logic to apply to Polyrepresentation. Later in the section on Future Research we outline alternative logical approaches already under development.

EMPIRICAL EVIDENCE SUPPORTING POLYREPRESENTATION

Early evidence of polyrepresentation-like retrieval phenomena is found in the literature and is briefly outlined below. Concurrent with the launch of the idea and hypothesis in the 1990s some experiments took place that were guided by common retrieval ideas giving support to the hypothesis, but not directly aiming at Polyrepresentation.

EXPERIMENTS NOT BASED DIRECTLY ON POLYREPRESENTATION

Based on a relevant seed document, in 1989 McCain had experimented with merging of citation databases (*Science Citation Index*) and an domain database (*Medline*), in order to test if documents defined by the citing publications and also found in the domain database were more topically relevant than each of the document sets separately. A bit later in 1994 Miranda Pao carried out *database fusion* experiments of the same kind. In all those cases the inner overlap proved to perform better than the constituting sets of documents. The experiments did not adhere to any explicit theory but was carried out mainly because *database fusion* in commercial online hosts was made technically possible and the idea that academic citations may reinforce potential topical relationships.

Earlier in 1987 Croft and Thomson constructed an experimental IR system named I^3R that fused two fundamental retrieval models: a probabilistic and a vector space model. The idea was to intersect the two models (or engines) for better precision and to apply their union to improve recall. Which of the two models to apply in a retrieval situation was determined by knowledge-based user modeling. This approach of what was to become known as *data fusion* proved well for the intersection, which essentially is an inner overlap of documents retrieved from two different algorithmic interpretations of their indexing features.

Searcher statements of their request were also experimented in combinations, e.g. by Belkin et al. (1995) who found that such combinations performed better than each single statement. Obviously, such request statements may only be available from the searcher in question after several iterations, not from the initiation of the IR interaction. Nevertheless the idea to extract information associated with the searcher situation seemed promising. Human relevance feedback on retrieved documents and combinations of algorithmic indexing weights were also shown to outperform the individual algorithms (Belkin et al, 2002; 2003).

Many other IR experiments are relevant for this discussion, but will be omitted here. One may, for instance, point to almost all data fusion experiments done from the mid-1990s. They are basically dealing with fusions of different search engines/retrieval models. In most such experiments only the final result of all the fused models are the findings that are published and discussed. However, as observed in some data fusion experiments based on Polyrepresentation the results of *intermediate combinations* may indeed be more powerful than the total one. This may be due to the fact that less-well performing retrieval models downgrade the combined outcome. When all models are fused the less performing ones participate - and combinations without them may thus perform better.

EXPERIMENTS BASED ON POLYREPRESENTATION

We divide the following experiments into groups according to the model, Figure 1. First, Experiments on the document space are discussed. This is followed by an outline of experiments with data fusion of IR models and IR interaction as process, incorporating contextual elements. Finally, we discuss polyrepresentation experiments associated with the searcher's retrieval and task situation - and point to future potentials for polyrepresentation theory.

POLYREPRESENTATION OF DOCUMENT SPACE

The McCain and Pao experiments with database fusions were re-done by Christoffersen (2004). in a much larger scale study with very positive results, seen from a polyrepresentation point of view.

Skov, Larsen and Ingwersen (2008) investigated combinations of query structures and document representations applying a rather small test collection consisting of 1200 documents, 29 search tasks and three-graded relevance assessments, but including all references and citation frequency for each document. The study tested: 1) query structure, i.e. natural language 'bag-of-words' mode versus query structure value-added by MeSH (Medical Subject Heading) terms as well as 2) the use of combinations of Reference title words; TI; AB; and DE terms. A total of 15 different overlap combinations were tested, see Figure 4.

	Natural language queries			Highly structured queries				
Overlap	# doc.	P all relevant	R all relevant	# doc	P all relevant	P highly relevant	R all relevant	R highly relevant
Ol 1 (ti/ab,mj,mn,rf)	126	41%	5%	58	69%	53%	4%	6%
Ol 2 (ti/ab, mj, mn)	668	13%	8%	100	42%	20%	4%	4%
Ol 3 (ti/ab, mj, rf)	101	48%	4%	66	79%	45%	5%	6%
Ol 4 (ti/ab, mn, rf)	240	29%	6%	68	62%	47%	4%	7%
Ol 5 (mj, mn, rf)	3	0	0	11	64%	45%	1%	1%
Ol 6 (ti/ab, mj)	702	12%	7%	131	45%	22%	5%	6%
Ol 7 (ti/ab, mn)	1761	9%	14%	210	27%	13%	5%	6%
Ol 8 (ti/ab, rf)	1528	9%	12%	162	27%	19%	4%	6%
Ol 9 (mj, mn)	141	6%	1%	42	26%	14%	1%	1%
Ol 10 (mj, rf)	6	33%	0	16	38%	19%	1%	1%
Ol 11 (mn, rf)	42	21%	1%	68	34%	16%	2%	2%
Ol 12 (ti/ab)	16201	2%	25%	770	12%	5%	8%	8%
Ol 13 (mj)	106	10%	1%	109	27%	12%	3%	3%
Ol 14 (mn)	603	4%	2%	336	17%	7%	5%	5%
Ol 15 (rf)	872	5%	4%	2458	6%	2%	12%	10%

Fig. 4. Precision (P) and Recall (R) results for 15 overlap (Ol) combinations of cognitive and functionally different search keys over structured and unstructured query types. 'mj': major MeSH terms; 'mn': minor MeSH terms. (From 2008).

The table, Figure 4, shows that the structured query types perform better on all combinations for precision, regardless if measured for highly relevant documents or in general. This was in line with the prediction made by Kekäläinen and Järvelin (2000). But the table also demonstrates that intermediate OL 3 performs better than the total OL 1 for the natural language *and* the structured query types on general precision. It is also evident that overlaps that combine index terms and author title/abstract terms or the functionally different reference title words provide the best performances. For the natural language queries it concerns OL 1 (total combination); OL 3 for any three-combination; and OL 10 for any two-fusion. This is almost the same for structured queries, except that OL 4/6 also perform very well. The reference title words seem to contribute positively in all their combinations - in line with what Garfield (1979; 1993) believed would strengthen IR performance.

Skov et al.'s findings strongly indicate that the more cognitively and functionally different the representations in overlaps, the higher the precision. Combinations with reference title terms outperformed other combinations as well as individual searches, but minor and major descriptor terms combined did not perform well (OL5 and OL9). Structured queries outperformed unstructured queries over all combinations. Adding weights to selected combinations busted such polyrepresentation combinations' performance in Top-10 rankings over natural language bag-of-words queries. However, P@5 was highest for this query type compared to any polyrepresentation combination. Re-ranking by citation frequency decreased performance slightly but the range of citations was small though!

Another way to apply citations and references in a polyrepresentation manner was tried out by Larsen (2002) following a so-called 'boomerang' principle. It implies to: 1) retrieve a set of documents by means of bag-of-words retrieval and polyrepresentation according to Figure 3, right hand side.; 2) apply the references in the set to go back in time and retrieve the documents cited; these can be ranked according to citation intensity; 3) move forward in time to all the documents citing the second set, including the initial one; 4) rank the documents according to a variety of parameters. The experiements did not show superior performance for the polyrepresentation mode compared to the simplistic and traditional natural language bag-of-words retrieval mode. The issue here is, among others, how far back to allow the references to be included in the second step. One way not tested so far would be to apply the citing half-life as limit. This line of research is under development.

POLYREPRESENTATION OF IR ENGINES

Figure 5 illustrates how data fusion of four algorithmically different IR models/search engines may result in several intermediate and total cognitive overlaps of documents retrieved by each engine. Obviously, for each engine Polyrepresentation principles might have been applied to the document representations and/or the searcher statements - see Figure 2.

Data fusion according to Polyrepresentation was tested by Larsen, Ingwersen and Lund (2009). It was discovered that the Polyrepresentation principle could be divided into two different modes: *Disjoint* (or restricted) overlaps, for which each document is only found in one overlap by means of 'not' logic (Boolean). In Figure 5 the disjoint principle implies that the documents in 'fuse4' are *not* also found as part of any 'fuse3' configuration. Each overlap is thus isolated (shown as shades of gray on figure 5).

Another way of generating polyrepresentation is *relaxed* (or traditional data fusion). Documents in 'fuse4' are also present in the 'fuse3' and 'fuse2' overlaps, providing a list of documents that may be ranked by weights according to their presence. In the initial polyrepresentation experiments the disjoint principle was followed. It became apparent that the relaxed principle provided more robust results, see Figure 6, which outline the experimental findings from the Larsen, Ingwersen and Lund (2009) experiments on data fusion in the TREC context.

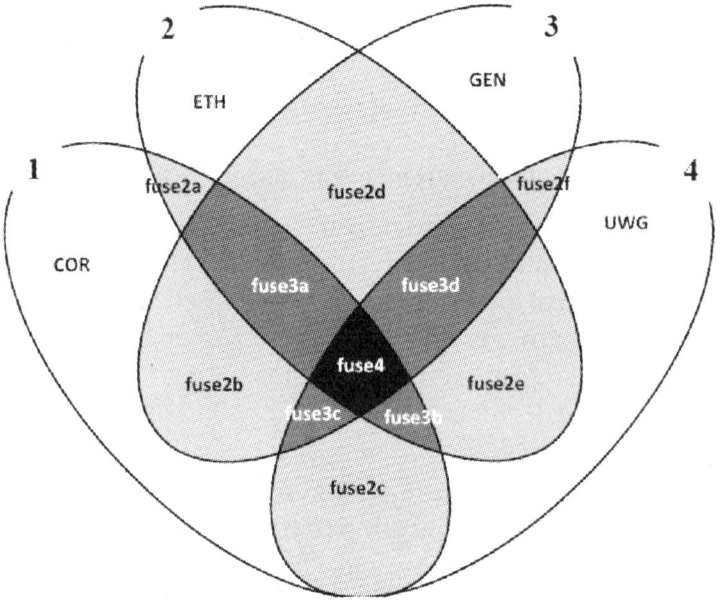

Fig. 5. Graphical illustration of polyrepresentation of four different retrieval models' search results in the form of disjoint overlapping documents (from Larsen, Ingwersen and Lund, 2009, p. 648).

The experiments applied 30 TREC 5 topics and the ad-hoc TREC retrieval and relevance data from four different IR models: two engines of the SMART (vector space) family, ETH and COR; one model based on Natural Language Processing algorithms (GEN); and one special algorithmic model (UWG). Figure 6 shows the retrieval performance at a cut-off value of 100 documents across the 30 topics. As in other polyrepresentation experiments overlaps of (cognitively) different *and* strong IR models show higher precision than the constituting models individually (e.g. ETH-UWG). However, not all overlaps are better than the best single retrieval model (UWG: 42.2/3 % precision). That depends on the familiarity and strength of the fused engines.

Combinations of TREC 5 IR models	Restricted Fusion: Fusion Name	Restricted Fusion: Precision	Restricted Fusion: Recall	Traditional Fusion: Fusion Name	Traditional Fusion: Precision	Traditional Fusion: Recall
ETH-GEN-UWG-COR	R-Fuse4	*0.482*	0.295	Fuse4	0.448	0.262
ETH-GEN-UWG	R-Fuse3d	*0.472*	0.308	Fuse3d	*0.463*	**0.271**
COR-GEN-UWG	R-Fuse3c	*0.472*	0.301	Fuse3c	0.458	0.268
COR-ETH-UWG	R-Fuse3b	0.444	**0.311**	Fuse3b	0.437	0.256
COR-ETH-GEN	R-Fuse3a	0.392*	0.303	Fuse3a	0.401	0.235
ETH-UWG	R-Fuse2e	*0.457*	**0.341**	Fuse2e	**0.456**	**0.267**
GEN-UWG	R-Fuse2f	0.445	0.323	Fuse2f	0.425	0.249
COR-UWG	R-Fuse2c	0.425	0.317	Fuse2c	0.431	0.252
ETH-GEN	R-Fuse2d	0.414*	0.318	Fuse2d	0.411	0.241
COR-ETH	R-Fuse2a	0.391*	0.304	Fuse2a	0.395	0.231
COR-GEN	R-Fuse2b	0.385*	0.301	Fuse2b	0.381	0.223
UWG		**0.423***	**0.323**		**0.422**	**0.246**
ETH		0.404*	**0.323**		0.404	0.236
GEN		0.347*	0.279		0.353*	0.206
COR		0.343*	0.274		0.343*	0.201

Fig. 6. data fusion results from Larsen, Ingwersen and Lund (2009). Figures in bold: best performance in type of overlap; in *italics* show statistical significance over *-marked values.

We observe that the 'restricted' data fusion mode shows a somewhat more blurred pattern than that shown by the 'relaxed/traditional' fusion mode (Figure 6, right hand side). We may further observe that (again) the intermediate fusion (3d: UWG-ETH-GEN) performs better than the total fusion of all four IR models. This is due to the weakness of the COR model and its only *functional difference* from ETH (vector space family).

Another aspect of fusion of many different search engines/retrieval models is demonstrated by Efron and Winget (2010) by introducing pseudo-relevance assessments based on Polyrepresentation principles in a TREC context. The idea was to replace the human relevance assessments, made in many participating laboratories' retrieval models according to pooling strategies, by simply pooling and weighting the retrieval results following Polyrepresentation principles. Documents found by several engines received higher weights according to different schemes. In this way the performance of each retrieval engine was measured against the pooled weighted list of documents, so to speak. Tests demonstrate that the final ranking of the retrieval models in between with respect to performance corresponds quite well to the ranking made by human relevance assessments.

Already in 2008 Baillie et al. had proposed that the pooling strategy applied in the TREC experiments favor retrieval based on Polyrepresentation. Hence, when re-applying TREC datasets and retrieval results in new (data fusion) experiments one would expect that Polyrepresentation to be superior.

POLYREPRESENTATION IN IR INTERACTION

The Glasgow IR group continued their relevance feedback experiments from 2002 and 2003 (Ruthven et al.), but adapted the Polyrepresentation approach in their later experiments. White et al (2005; 2006; 2006b) tested various ways of applying implicit *relevance feedback* in interface designs captured from searchers through the IR interaction process. White (2005; 2006) based several of his experiments on simulations on users, of which the best solutions were further tested with real test persons in the laboratory. White proposed to apply "[content-rich] search interfaces that implement an aspect of polyrepresentation theory, and are capable of displaying multiple representations of the retrieved documents simultaneously in the results interface" (White, 2006, p. 1185). The prototype interface implemented a *progressive revealment* strategy where searchers could access an increasing amount of retrieved document content by following interactive relevance paths between different representations created from the same document. Such representations were top-ranking sentences from a retrieved document, its title, its query-biased summary (commonly four sentences), single summary sentences, or summary sentences in context. By hovering over specific representations or by clicking on icons the interface guided the searcher further on, and the traversal of these paths was then used by an IRF model to select terms for query modification (White, 2006, p. 1187). Three 'simulated search' scenarios (Borlund, 2003) were tested for retrieval performance by means of searcher simulations of all possible combinations of representations and paths available. The best performing combination of representations consisted of document title, its query-biased summary and summary sentence in context (Larsen, Ingwersen and Kekäliänen, 2006).

The IR interaction process is valuable because it may supply different kinds of information back to the IR system from the searcher and or his/her contextual situation. Bogers and van den Bosch experimented with different algorithms for *recommender systems*. Rating and recommendations from many searchers over time constitute a kind of a *social utility* indicator - see Lecture 2 - which is a useful tool for some retrieval approaches. They experimented with a variety of different recommender approaches and found, in line with Polyrepresentation theory, that the best performance was done by *combinations* of very (cognitively) different recommender algorithms.

Also by application of IR interaction information Beckers (2009) investigated information seeking strategies and the use of Polyrepresentation in connection with book retrieval. He proposed to "[support] both polyrepresentation of information objects and multiple information seeking strategies in order to cope with the shortcomings of most current retrieval systems." (p. 58). Beckers applied Amazon.com and Library Thing representations and ratings on the document side. He proposed a four-step model for the IR interaction process, taking into account the polyrepresentative nature of the documents and design of the interface: Selection; Organization; Projection; and Visualization.

POLYREPRESENTATION OF THE COGNITIVE SPACE

There are probably much more potential in the IR

interaction process than demonstrated above for capture of user-centered and contextual data. First we discuss the experiments by Kelly and Fu (2007) directly aimed at the searcher's cognitive space. In the section on Future Polyrepresentation Research we refer to recent developments in this respect (Lykke et al., 2010).

Kelly and Fu (2007): made use of the Hard track of TREC generating 45 'topics' by 13 test persons who also made binary relevance assessments for their own topics. At the time of generating the topic each test person was asked four questions concerning the search job situation through an online questionnaire

Q1: Times in the past searching topic?

Q2: Describe what you already know about topic

Q3: Why do you want to know about this topic? - the underlying work task

Q4: Please input any additional keywords that describe your topic.

The second question concerns representation of the searcher's *knowledge state* concerning the topic; Q3 asks to the underlying *reason* for seeking information on the topic, e.g. a task description; and Q4 asks if the searcher have some more pertinent information to provide. In addition the usual TREC topic title (= the request) exists with a description of what is regarded relevant documents. In total four functionally different representations of the search situation is thus provided by the searcher for each topic.

Kelly and Fu made use of a standard experimental probabilistic retrieval engine (BM25) and applied MAP and T-tests as performance measure and statistical validation tool. Their baseline run (BL) was made on the request title and topic description. Independent variables were a: 1) range of pseudo-relevance feedback runs (BL rank1-5 regarded relevant; BL rank 1-10 regarded relevant ...); 2) combinations of Q2-Q4 statements on top of the BL, used as query modification tool. Kelly and Fu made use of the unionof the BL and the Q versions, implying a recall-like mode of retrieval (Set A+B), with search key duplets in the combined versions receiving higher weights, see Figure 7.

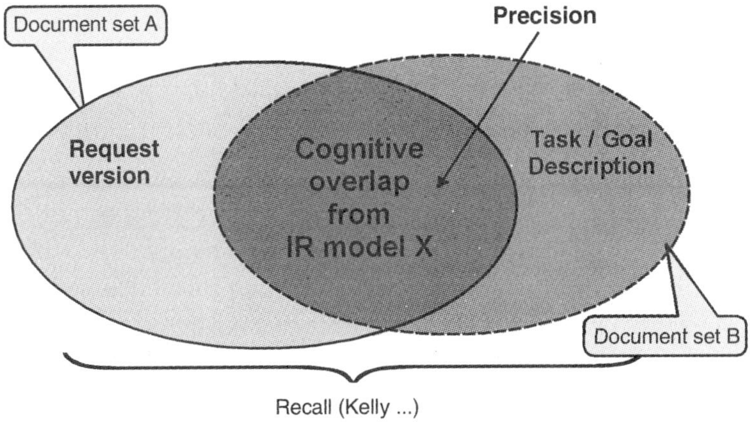

Fig. 7. Illustration of documents retrieved by overlaps of different representations of a searcher's cognitive structures by one IR model/ engine. Intersection implies precision retrieval mode.

The main findings showed that considerable variations existed between and within the different request forms in terms of number of meaningful terms applied by the test persons; on average the figures are: BL (request topic): 9.33 terms; Q2 (what): 18.16 terms; Q3 (why): 10.67; and Q 4 add keys): 2.33 terms. Most importantly: most pseudo relevance runs (except for pseudo50) performed less well than the baseline (.284). All single and combined Q2-3 versions performed better than BL but only the *fusion of Q2-3* could beat BL plus all kinds of pseudo-relevance feedback variations. In general a strong correlation was found between query length and performance. This latter finding is not surprising from an IR perspective, with longer queries commonly performing better than shorter ones.

FUTURE POLYREPRESENTATION RESEARCH

Many aspects of IR can be dealt with through Polyrepresentation. Here we have reviewed a selection of studies of some of the possibilities. For each media, genre, domain and document type there exist sets of cognitive actors that may contribute a diversity of interpretations of documents, requests, assessments, or other retrieval phenomena. Some are quite different, being *cognitively* different, others derive from the same (group of) actors, thus being *functionally* different.

Time has an important impact on Polyrepresentation. For the social utility types of interpretations, such as rating/ recommendations or use of citations/references it is a question about how far back in time one wishes to analyze the social phenomena. The underlying rationale for the ratings, recommendations or citations may have changed radically. This can be seen in the *use of concepts* and the change of vocabulary over time. The same concept may indeed exist, but under a new key (term), or a concept has disappeared but the key (term) still exists - but with a different meaning.

Thus, when searching a database using Polyrepresentation, the *age* of the involved information objects is central - but hitherto almost not studied. The intuition is that all the representations, Figure 2, should be *concurrent manifestations* rather than showing large temporal variation.

Another central facet of polyrepresentation lies in the *weighting* of the different representations. Hitherto the studies assumed equal weighting for all the participating representations. However, as recently shown by Lioma et al. (2010) other than standard (true/false) logics are indeed available, e.g. *probabilistic* logic or *subjective* logic. The former takes into account ignorance and uncertainty when assessing propositions. The latter takes into account that beliefs are held by individuals and operates on subjective beliefs about the world in the presence of uncertain or partially incomplete evidence.

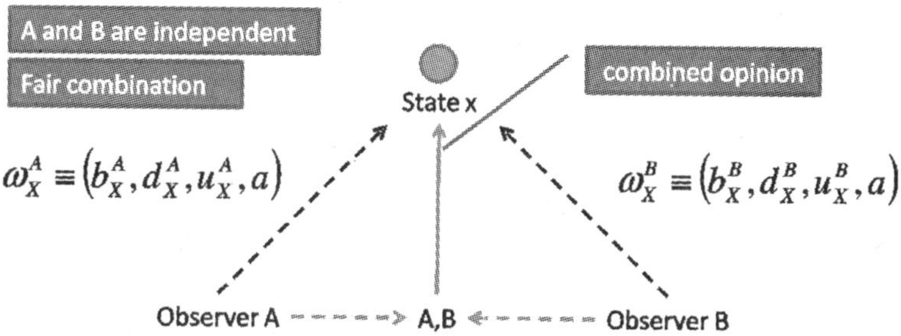

$$\omega_X^A \equiv (b_X^A, d_X^A, u_X^A, a) \qquad \omega_X^B \equiv (b_X^B, d_X^B, u_X^B, a)$$

$$\omega_X^{A,B} \equiv (\omega_X^A \oplus \omega_X^B)$$

Fig. 8. Subjective logic. Consensus between independent opinions (From Lioma et al., 2010, p.132).

Figure 8 displays how subjective logic may operate with equal weights given to the two different observations (representations in a Polyrepresentation sense) providing a consensus opinion in a cognitive overlap. The effect of the consensus operator is to reduce uncertainty. This is the same as has been done in the standard Polyrepresentation studies discussed above. But this may not always be appropriate, according to Lioma et al. (2010), for instance, in a topical web search where the background knowledge may introduce topic drift.

Consequently, one may wish to experiment with *un-equality* between opinions (or representations). The effect of the recommendation operator is to bias the combination in favour of one representation, and thus facilitating uses of contextual evidence. One may argue that when an indexer (or indexing algorithm) makes use of an ontology designed by other actors prior to the event, there exists a dependency between the indexer and the ontology construct and entities (e.g. terms). Similarly with respect to the citing document titles and abstracts. They can be seen as contextual (temporal event) and dependent of the document cited. Hence one should add higher weights to such opinions.

A different track is to apply the quantum-inspired geometrical retrieval framework, as suggested by Fromholz et al. (2010, p. 115).

"Multiple representations of documents, like user-given reviews or the actual document content, can give evidence towards certain facets of relevance. In this respect polyrepresentation of documents, where such evidence is combined, is a crucial concept to estimate the relevance of a document. [The] paper ... discusses how a geometrical retrieval framework inspired by quantum mechanics can be extended to support polyrepresentation. We show by example how different representations of a document can be modeled in a Hilbert space, similar to physical systems known from quantum mechanics. We further illustrate how these representations are combined by means of the tensor product to support polyrepresentation, and discuss the case that representations of documents are not independent from a user point of view. Besides giving a principled framework for polyrepresentation, the potential of this approach is to capture and formalise the complex interdependent relationships that the different representations can have between each other."

Evidently there is capacity in Polyrepresentation for developments that may enrich IR research. There is a need for studying which combinations of representations that in any given case of media, genre, domain and document type may enhance the most the performance and end result for the searcher. It seems evident from the studies described above, and from the general experience of data fusion research, that low-performing engine/actor representations will reduce performance. So, the future application of Polyrepresentation should make use of the best performing entities/ representations combined. This also implies that *intermediate combinations* of representations, such as observed in our data fusion studies, may very well be better performers than the total combination of several representations.

We need to carry out more robust tests including bigger and more recent data sets; graded relevance; real searchers, non-textual material; and contextual information (like the implicit relevance feedback studies by White et al.) and citation/reference data.

Some of these requirements have been met in the *I*Search test collection, which currently is under development (Lykke et al., 2010). *I*Search comprises the integration of 160,000 journal articles in full text PDF and their abstracts, plus additional 275,000 abstracts and references/citations of articles, all from the arxiv.com portal on Physics and Computer Science. In addition the collection includes 18,000 book records from research libraries and is based on 65 real research tasks represented by 5 situational facets constructed by Physics PhD students and staff at universities who also preformed the four-scale graded relevance assessments.

We hope to publish further polyrepresentation and integrated search findings based on this collection in the future.

References

Adamic, L. (1999). "The small world Web." *Lecture Notes in Computer Science*, 1696, 443-452.

Aguillo, I. F. (1998). "STM information on the Web and the development of new Internet RandD databases and indicators." *Online Information* 98, *Proceedings*, 239-243.

Allen, E.S., Burke, J.M., Welch, M.E., Rieseberg, L.H. (1999). „How reliable is science information on the Web?" *Science*, 402, 722.

Almind, T. C., and Ingwersen, P. (1997). "Infometric analyses on the World Wide Web, Methodological approaches to 'webometrics'." *Journal of Documentation*, 53(4), 404-426.

Baillie, M., Azzopardi, L., and Ruthven, I. (2008). "Evaluating epistemic uncertainty under incomplete assessments." *Information Processing and Management*, 44(2), 811–837.

Bar-Ilan, J. (1997). "The "mad cow disease," Usenet newsgroups and bibliometric laws." *Scientometrics*, 39(1), 29-55.

Bar-Ilan, J. (2004). "The use of Web search engines in information science research." *Annual Review of Information Science and Technology*, 38, 231-288.

Beckers, T. (2009). "Supporting Polyrepresentation and Information Seeking Strategies." In *Proceedings of the 3rd Symposium on Future Directions in Information Access* (FDIA), 56–61.

Belkin, N.J., Kantor, P., Fox, E. and Shaw, J.A. (1995). "Combining the evidence of multiple query representations for information retrieval." *Information Processing and Management, 31,* 431-448.

Björneborn, L. (2001). "Small-world linkage and co-linkage." *Proceedings of the 12th ACM Conference on Hypertext,* 133-134.

Bjorneborn, L., and Ingwersen, P. (2001). "Perspectives of webometrics." *Scientometrics,* 50(1), 65-82.

Björneborn, L., and Ingwersen, P. (2004). „Towards a basic framework for webometrics." *Journal of American Society for Information Science and Technology,* 55(14), 1216-1227.

Bogers, T. and van den Bosch, A. (2011). Fusing Recommendations for Social Bookmarking Websites. *International Journal of Electronic Commerce,* 15(3), 33–75.

Borlund, P. (2003): "The IIR evaluation model : a framework for evaluation of interactive information retrieval systems." *Information Research,* 8(3), paper no. 152. [http://informationr.net/ir/8-3/paper152.html]

Brin, S., and Page, L. (1998). „The anatomy of a large scale hypertextual web search engine." *Computer Networks and ISDN Systems,* 30(1-7), 107-117.

Broder, A. et al. (2000). "Graph structure in the Web." *Computer Networks,* 33(1-6), 309-320.

Chavan, V. .S and Ingwersen, P. (2010). "Towards a Data Publishing Framework for Primary Biodiversity Data, Challenges and Potentials." *BMC Bioinformatics,* 2009, 10 (Suppl. 14),S2.

Christensen, F.H., Ingwersen, P., and Wormell, I. (1997). „Online determination of the journal impact factor and its international properties." *Scientometrics*, 40(3), 529-540.

Christoffersen, M. (2004). "Identifying core documents with a multiple evidence relevance filter." *Scientometrics, 61*(3), 385-394.

Chu, H., He, S., and Thelwall, M. (2002). "Library and information science schools in Canada and USA, A Webometric perspective." *Journal of Education for Library and Information Science*, 43(2).

Croft, W.B. and Thomson, R.H. (1987). "I3R: A new approach to the design of document retrieval systems." *Journal of the American Society for Information Science, 38*(6), 389-404.

De Solla Price, D. (1986). "Little Science, Big Science ... and Beyond." With foreword by Robert Merton and Eugene Garfield. Washington, Columbia University Press.

Efron, M. and Winget, M. (2010). "Query polyrepresentation for ranking retrieval systems without relevance judgments. *Journal of the American Society for Information Science and Technology*, 61(6), 1081-1091.

Elleby, A., and Ingwersen, P. (2010). "Publication Point Indicators, A Comparative Case Study of two Publication Point Systems and Citation Impact in an Interdisciplinary Context." *Journal of Informetrics*, 2010, 4, 512-523.

Elsevier. "Scopus". Available at, http,//www.scopus.com/

Frommholz, I., Larsen, B., Piwowarski, B., Lalmas, M., Ingwersen, P. and van Rijsbergen, K. (2010). "Supporting polyrepresentation in a quantum-inspired geometrical retrieval framework. In: Belkin, N. J. and Kelly, D. (eds.), *IIiX'10 Proceeding of the Third Symposium on Information Interaction in Context, New Brunswick, NJ, USA, August 18-21, 2010*.. New York, ACM Press, 115-124.

Garfield, E. (1979). "Citation indexing: Its theory and application in science, technology and humanities." New York, NY: Wiley [Reprinted by ISI Press, 1983].

Garfield, E. (1993). "KeyWord Okys (TM): Algorithmic derivative indexing." *Journal of the American Society for Information Science*, 44(5), 298–299.

Global Biodiversity Information Facility (GBIF) - available at, http,//data.gbif.org

Glänzel, W. (2004). Keynote Lecture at the Nordic Bibliometric Meeting, sepetmber. Umeå University, Sweden.

Granovetter, M.S. (1973). "The strength of weak ties." *American Journal of Sociology*, 78(6), 1360-1380.

Heidorn, P.B. (2008). "Shedding light on the dark data in the long tail of science." *Library Trends*, 57(2). [https,//www.ideals.uiuc.edu/bitstream/handle/2142/9127/Heidorn_LongTail_PreprintwEdits.doc.pdf?sequence=7].

Holmberg, K. (2009). "Webometric Network Analysis, Mapping Cooperation and Geopolitical Connections between Local Government Administration on the Web". Doctoral Dissertation. Åbo, Åbo Akademi University Press. Available at, http,//urn.fi/URN,ISBN,978-951-765-511-8

Holmberg, K. (2010). "Web Impact Factors, A significant contribution to Webometric research." In, Larsen, B. (ed.), *The Janus-faced Scholar, A festschrift in Honor of Peter Ingwersen*. Royal School Of Library and Information Science and ISSI, 127-134.

Ingwersen, P. (1992)."Information Retrieval Interaction". London, Taylor Graham.

Ingwersen, P. (1996). "Cognitive perspectives of information retrieval interaction: Elements of a cognitive IR theory." *Journal of Documentation*, 52, 3–50.

Ingwersen, P. (1998). "The calculation of Web Impact Factors." *Journal of Documentation*, 54, 236-243

Ingwersen, P. and Chavan, V. S. (2011). "Indicators for the Data Usage Index (DUI): an incentive for publishing primary biodiversity data through global information infrastructure." *BMC Bioinformatics* (in press).

Ingwersen, P., and Järvelin, K. (2005). "The Turn, Integration of Information Seeking and Retrieval in Context." Heidelberg, Springer.

Ingwersen, P., Larsen, B., and Kekäläinen, J. (2006). " The polyrepresentation continuum in IR." In, Ruthven, I., et al. (eds.), *Information Interaction in Context, Proceedings of the International Symposium on Information Interaction in Context* (IiiX 2006). Copenhagen; New York, Royal School of Library and Information Science / ACM Press, 148-162.

Ingwersen, P., Larsen, B, Rousseau, R., and Russell, J. (2001). "The publication-citation matrix and its derived quantities." *Chinese Science Bulletin*, 46(6), 524-528.

Ingwersen, P., Schneider, J.W., Scharff, M., and Larsen, B. (2007). " A national research profile-based Immediacy Index and citation ratio indicator for research evaluation." In, Torres-Salinas, D., and Moed, H.F. (eds.), *Proceedings of the 11th ISSI Conference*. Madrid, CINDOC, 864-865.

Järvelin, K., and Persson, O. (2008). "The DCI index, Discounted cumulated impact-based research evaluation." *Journal of the American Society for Information Science andTechnology*, 59(9), 1433–1440.

Järvelin, K., and Kekäläinen, J. (2002). "Cumulated gain-based evaluation of IR techniques". *ACM Transactions on Information Systems (ACM TOIS)*, *20*(4), 422-446.

Jepsen, E.T., Seiden, P., Ingwersen, P., Björneborn, L., and Borlund, P. (2004). „Characteristics of scientific Web publications, Preliminary data gathering and analysis." *Journal of American Society for Information Science and Technology*, 55(14), 1239-1249.

Jacso, P. (2008). "Google Scholar revisited." *Online Information Review*, 32(1), 102-114. Available, http,//www.emerald insight.com/Insight/ViewContentServlet?Filename= Published/EmeraldFullTextArticle/Articles/ 2640320108.html

Kekäläinen, J. and Järvelin, K. (2000). "The co-effects of query structure and expansion on retrieval performance in probabilistic text retrieval." *Information Retrieval*, 1(4), 329-344.

Kelly, D., and Fu, X. (2007). "Eliciting better information need descriptions from users of information search systems." *Information Processing and Management*, 43(1), 30–46.

Kleinberg, J., and Lawrence, S. (2001). "The structure of the Web." *Science*, 294, 1849-1850.

Kousha, K., and Thelwall, M. (2007). "How is Science cited on the Web? A classification of Google unique Web citations." *Journal of American Society for Information Science and Technology*, 58(11), 1631-1644.

Larsen, B. (2002). "Exploiting citation overlaps for information retrieval: Generating a boomerang effect from the network of scientific papers." *Scientometrics*, *54*(2), 155-178.

Larsen, B., Ingwersen, P. and Kekäläinen, J. (2006). "The Polyrepresentation continuum in IR." In: Information Interaction in Context: Proceedings of the First IIiX Symposium, Copenhagen. ACM Press, 148-162.

Larsen, B., Ingwersen, P. and Lund, B. (2009)." Data Fusion According to the Principle of Polyrepresentation". ." *Journal of American Society for Information Science and Technology*, 60(4), 646-654.

Lawrence, S., and Giles, C. L. (1999). "Accessibility and distribution of information on the Web." *Nature*, 400, 107-110.

Li, X.M., Thelwall, M., Musgrove, P., and Wilkinson, D. (2003). "The relationship between the WIFs or inlinks of Computer Science Departments in UK and their RAE ratings or research productivities in 2001." *Scientometrics*, 57(2), 239-255.

Lioma, C., Larsen, B., Schütze, H. and Ingwersen, P. (2010). "A Subjective Logic Formalization of the Principle of Polyrepresentation for Information Needs." In, Belkin, N. J. and Kelly, D. (ed.), *IIiX'10 Proceeding of the Third Symposium on Information Interaction in Context, New Brunswick, NJ, USA, August 18-21, 2010*. New York, ACM, 125-134.

Lykke, M., Larsen, B., Lund, H. and Ingwersen, P. (2010). "Developing a Test Collection for the Evaluation of Integrated Search. In: *Advances in Information Retrieval." Proceedings of 32nd European Conference on IR Research*, ECIR 2010, Milton Keynes, UK, March 28-31, (p. 627-630). Berlin, Springer. DOI- 10.1007/978-3-642-12275-0_63.

McCain, K.W. (1989). "Descriptor and citation retrieval in the medicine behavioral sciences literature: Retrieval overlaps and novelty distribution." *Journal of the American Society for Information Science, 40*, 110-114.

Moed, H.F. (2005). "Citation analysis in research evaluation". Dordrecht, Springer.

Moed, H., de Bruin, R.E., and van Leuven, Th.N. (1995). "New bibliometric tools for the assessment of national research performance, database description, overview of indicators and first applications." *Scientometrics*, 33, 381-442.

Nielsen Blog Pulse; available, http,//www.blogpulse.com/tools.html

Pao, M. (1994). "Relevance odds of retrieval overlaps from seven search fields." *Information Processing and Management, 30*(3), 305-314.

Rao, I.K.R. (2008). "Growth of Literature and Measures of Scientific Productivity - Scientometric Models." New Delhi, Ess Ess Publications for Serada Ranganathan Endowment for Library Science, Bangalore.

Ruthven, I., Lalmas, M. and van Rijsbergen, K. (2002). "Ranking expansion terms with partial and ostensive evidence. " In: Bruce, H. et al. (Eds.) *Emerging Frameworks and Methods. Proceedings of the 4th International Conference on Conceptions of Library and Information Science (CoLIS 4)*, July 21-25, 2002, Seattle, USA. Greenwood Village, CO: Libraries Unlimited, 199-220.

Ruthven, I., Lalmas, M. and van Rijsbergen, K. (2003). "Incorporating user search behaviour into relevance feedback. " *Journal of the American Society for Information Science and Technology, 54*(6), 529-549.

Schneider, J.W. (2009). "An outline of the bibliometric indicator used for performance-based funding of research institutions in Norway." *European Political Science*, 8(3), 364-378.

Skov, M., Larsen, B. and Ingwersen, P. (2008). "Inter and intra-document contexts applied in polyrepresentation for best match IR." *Information Processing and Management*, 44(5), 1673–1683.

Smith, A. G. (1999). "**A** tale of two Webspaces, Comparing sites using Web impact factors." *Journal of*

Documentation, 55(5), 577-592.

Smith, A. G., and Thelwall, M. (2002). "Web impact factors for Australasian universities." *Scientometrics*, 54(3), 363-380.

Swanson, D.R. (1986)." Undiscovered public knowledge." *Library Quarterly*, 56(2), 103-118.

Thelwall, M. (2000). "Web impact factors and search engine coverage." *Journal of Documentation*, 56, 185-189.

Thelwall, M. (2002). "Conceptualizing documentation on the Web, An evaluation of different heuristic-based models for counting links between university Web sites." *Journal of American Society for Information Science and Technology*, 53(12), 995-1005.

Thelwall, M. (2003). "Web use and peer interconnectivity metrics for academic Web sites. *Journal of Information Science*, 29(1), 1-10.

Thelwall, M., Vaughan, L., and Björneborn, L. (2005). "Webometrics." *Annual Review of Information Science and Technology*, Chapter 3, 81-135.

Thelwall, M., and Harries, G. (2004). "Do better scholars' web publications have significantly higher online impact?" *Journal of the American Society for Information Science and Technology*, 55(2), 149-159.

Thomson-Reuters. "Web of Science". Available at, http,// www.isiknowldge.com/

Ulrich Database, Available at, http,//ulrichsweb.com/

van Raan, A.F.J. (1999). "Advanced Bibliometric methods for the evaluation of universities". *Scientometrics*, 45(3), 417-423.

White, R.W. (2006). "Using searcher simulations to redesign a polyrepresentative implicit feedback interface." *Information Processing and Management*, vol. 42(5), 1185-1202.

White, R.W., Jose, J.M. and Ruthven, I. (2006). "An implicit feedback approach for interactive information retrieval." *Information Processing and Management*,vol. 42(1), 166-190.

White, R.W., Ruthven, I. and Jose, J.M. and van Rijsbergen, C.J. (2005). "Evaluating implicit feedback models using searcher simulations." *ACM Transactions on Information Systems*, 23(3), 325-361.

Yahoo Site Explorer available at : http://siteexplorer.search.yahoo.com/new

Index

C